ECONOMICS
An Examination of Scarcity
Adam Smith's Micro to
Current U.S. Macro

By Stephen K. Happel

ARIZONA STATE UNIVERSITY

THOMAS HORTON AND DAUGHTERS
26662 S. New Town Drive
Sun Lakes, AZ 85248
480-895-0480

This book is dedicated to my wife Elizabeth and my children Graydon, Sarah, and Margaret. I am also deeply indebted to my economic mentors E. Roy Weintraub, Joseph J. Spengler, and Richard Renner. And I must thank Mylo Reilly, Helen Rubio, and Vicenta Bonnit for their diligent attempts to read my writing while repeatedly retyping the manuscript.

Library of Congress Catalog Number 00-134179

ISBN 0-913878-62-6

Printed in the USA

Typography by Greg Swann Typography & Graphics

ECONOMICS
An Examination
of Scarcity

Adam Smith's Micro to

Current U.S. Macro

TABLE OF CONTENTS

Chapter One: Why People Hate Economics 1
A.   The Basic Perspective of Modern Economics 2
B.   The Remaining Chapters 3

Chapter Two: Adam Smith, Micro vs. Macro,
and Alerts to Modern Economic Thought......................... 5
A.   Adam Smith and Key Ideas from the *Wealth of Nations*........... 6
B.   Microeconomics, Macroeconomics, and Constant
     Conflict Between the Individual and the Group................. 11
C.   Three Additional Alerts to Modern Economic Thought 14
     1.   Free: The Most Dangerous Word in Economics
          and Perhaps the Entire English Language.................. 14
     2.   Economic Theories Argued Against the
          Backdrop of Contemporary Life........................... 15
     3.   Paradoxes Left and Right 16

Chapter Three: The Glorious Insights of
Free-Market Microeconomic Thought............................. 17
A.   Alfred Marshall and Basic Laws of Microeconomics............. 19
     1.   Marginalism and Equimarginalism........................ 20
     2.   The Law of Opportunity Cost, Plus the Notion of Sunk Cost.. 22
     3.   The Law of Diminishing Physical
          Returns and Related Per-Unit Costs...................... 24
     4.   Price Determination by Demand and Supply 27
          (1) The Law of Demand! 28
          (2) The Law of Supply? 29
          (3) The Two Blades of A Scissors:
               Demand and Supply Determine Price 31
B.   Externalities and the Coase Theorem 35
C.   Monopolies and Schumpeter's Forces of Creative Destruction....... 37
D.   Flows of Knowledge and Hayek's Insights 41
E.   Final Remarks... 43
F.   Appendix 3A: The U.S. Road and Driving Market 44
G.   Appendix 3B: Allocation of Faculty Offices 46
H.   Appendix 3C: Ticket Scalping............................... 53

Table of Contents

I.   Appendix 3D: The Chicago-Columbia Approach
     to Fertility and Becker's Rotten Kid Theorem 57

Chapter Four: Pricing Decisions by Firms ....
A.   Foundations 60
     1.   Demand Elasticities and Marginal Revenue 60
     2.   Marginal Costs, Average Costs, and Economic Profits or Losses . 66
B.   Micro Pricing Models of the Firm. 67
     1.   Pure Competition 68
     2.   Monopolistic Competition. 69
     3.   Oligopoly 71
     4.   Nondiscriminating Pure Monopoly 73
     5.   Price Discriminating Monopolies By Degrees 74
C.   Extensions   77
     1.   Incremental Versus Full Cost Pricing. 77
     2.   Pricing a New Product: Skimming Versus Penetration 78
     3.   Multiproduct Pricing: Equimarginalism Versus Loss Leaders . 78
     4.   Transfer Pricing of Inputs Within the Firm 79
D.   Concluding Remarks 80

Chapter Five: The Technical Transition from
Microeconomics to Macroeconomics 81
A.   Money: It's Not the Root of All Evil 82
     1.   Properties and Functions of Money. 82
     2.   General History of Money to the Time of Adam Smith 83
     3.   Critical Themes in the Monetary History of the U.S. 86
     4.   The U.S. from the 1650's to 1907. 86
          (1) American Revolution to the War of 1812. 86
          (2) 1812 to 1861: Times to Romp, Stomp, and Romp Again 88
          (3) 1861 to 1907: National Banks,
               Deflation, and The Great Panic. 90
     5.   The Creation of the Federal Reserve System in
          1913 and Subsequent Modifications. 92
     6.   U.S. Monetary History: 1914 to the Present 95
          (1) The Crash of 1929 through Bretton Woods and World War II . 96
          (2) 1946 to the Present: Regulation Versus Deregulation 99
     7.   Definitions of U.S. Monetary Aggregates. 102

B. Measuring the Flows of Output and Income:
   The National Product Accounts. 105
    1. The Definitions of GNP and GDP. 105
    2. The Expenditures Approach: C+I+G+(X-M). 106
    3. The Income Approach: W+R+i+π+CCA+IBT 107
    4. Alternative Measures of Welfare Beyond GDP. 108
    5. Nominal Versus Real GDP. 109
C. The Inherent Stability of Capitalism at
   Full Employment and Say's Law. 110
    1. The U.S. Labor Force and Definitions of Unemployment. 111
    2. Say's Law of Markets: Early Advocates and Major Critics. . . . 111
D. The Equation of Exchange 113
E. Concluding Remarks 114

Chapter Six: It's a Macroeconomic Jungle Out There!. 115
A. Personal Outlook 116
B. The Left and Right: Economic Liberals
   Versus Economic Conservatives. 118
C. Ten Macroeconomic Schools of Thought 120
    1. Adam Smith and His Classical Disciples. 120
    2. Swinging to the Far Left: Malthus,
      Neo-Malthusians, Marx-Engels, and Neo-Marxians. 122
    3. Founding British Keynesians 127
    4. Marshallian Macroeconomics. 128
      (1) The Pigou Effect. 130
      (2) Irving Fisher: A Compensated Dollar and the Fisher Effect. 131
    5. The Founding British Keynesians Again 132
    6. Early American Keynesians 136
    7. Post-Eclectic Keynesians. 139
    8. The Chicago School and Monetarism 140
    9. The Rational Expectations School. 145
    10. The Supply-Sider Perspective. 146
    11. The Far Right: The Austrian School. 148
D. Concluding Remarks 150
E. Appendix 5A: Recipients of the Nobel Prize
   in Economic Science: 1969-2000. 151
F. Appendix 5B: Recipients of the John Bates Clark Medal: 1947-2000 . 155

Table of Contents

G. Appendix 5C: Chairs of the Council of
    Economics Advisors (CEA): 1946-2000. 158

Chapter Seven: Looking at the Future of the U.S. Economy 160
A.   Four Major Forecasting Techniques 161
     1.   Mechanical Extrapolation 161
     2.   Barometric Methods. 162
     3.   Surveys or Opinion Polls 162
     4.   Econometric Modeling. 163
B.   How Modern Economics Has Convinced Me 164
C.   U.S. Demographic Patterns in Relation to the Economy 166
     1.   Working Age Groups and Inflation. 166
     2.   The Fifty-and-Older Population 168
     3.   Three "Generations" Since 1946 170
     4.   Harry Dent's Demographic Viewpoint 171
D.   The U.S. Economy and Presidential Administrations Since 1946 173
     1.   Averages Since 1946 175
     2.   Truman Years: 1946-1952 175
     3.   Eisenhower Years: 1953-1960 176
     4.   Kennedy-Johnson Years: 1961-1968 177
     5.   Nixon-Ford Years: 1969-1976. 179
     6.   Carter Years: 1977-1980 180
     7.   Reagan Years: 1981-1988 181
     8.   Bush Years: 1989-1992 183
     9.   Clinton Years: 1993-1999 184
E.   The U.S. Economy Over the Next Decade. 185
F.   Closing Comments 189

Bibliography 190

Subject Index 195

Author Index 198

To study music, we must first
learn the rules. To create
music, we must forget them.
—Aaron Copeland

CHAPTER ONE

WHY PEOPLE HATE ECONOMICS

Economics! Is there any "science" more disdained? A noted playwright laments that economists, when laid end-to-end, never reach a conclusion. Lyndon Johnson pleads for more one-handed economists because he is so tired of hearing, "On the one hand this, but on the other hand that." And there is the story about the forecasting job at a local bank going to the economist who, when asked what is three times seven, replies nineteen, which turned out to be the closest from all those interviewed.

Both undergraduate and graduate students frequently become exasperated by the terminology and logical complexity. They go into shock seeing graph after graph and hearing straight lines called "curves". We economists are known to insist that other disciplines are wrong in their social analysis and may not even understand their own methodology at times! Rather arrogantly, we point to the Council of Economic Advisors and to a Nobel award in economics. It may be hard to accept, but modern economic thought, in a very real sense, dominates day-to-day life in the U.S.

Modern economics is difficult because it has its own language, sets of rules and assumptions for analyzing issues. It demands precision. Before you can free-style, you must do the compulsories. It's not been called the "dismal science" for nothing.

However, once you understand the basic ideas, assumptions, and logic of modern economics, you have an extremely

1

powerful framework from which to confront both immediate and more long-term problems. The logic can be harsh, especially to well-intentioned individuals who believe that they know what is "best" for society in situations of scarcity. Yet it also allows you to see through the fuzzy thinking or pure emotion that cause the "economically-deprived" to go astray constantly. Of course I am biased, but nowhere will you gain more valuable insights into the "ordinary business of life" than through modern economics.

The Basic Perspective of Modern Economics

By overwhelming consensus, modern economics began with the appearance of Adam Smith's *Wealth of Nations* in 1776. This was the era of Newton and Calvin, great intellectuals struggling with religion, science, and humans place in the universe. Risk and uncertainty were coming under greater control through management techniques including insurance, annuities, organized equity markets, and futures trading. Capitalism was emerging as an economic system.

Smith wanted to create more national wealth — more goods and services — in the context of an ordered, moral society. His emphasis was on equilibrium — states of rest — based upon laws of nature, rather than upon chaotic change and highly disruptive shocks. Newton's vision of God as a watchmaker, who winds the fine mechanism of the universe and then sets it in motion, was intertwined with Calvin's moral principles of grace, hard-work, and thrift in Smith's *laissez-faire*, free-market arguments.

The basic perspective of modern economics has remained the same since the time of Smith. It continues to stress three themes:

- Change, while inevitable, can be channeled or harnessed into increased national wealth under the right conditions, and the world can be best characterized by equilibrium conditions and adjustments from one steady state to another.

- All rational individuals pursue their own unlimited self-interests. Irrational individuals are few in number and are those who can't or won't take care of themselves.
- Because of the binding constraints of nature and the physical world, unlimited human desires mean constant scarcity. This is true for individuals and for societies as a whole. The fundamental definition of economics is THE STUDY OF SCARCITY.

Even with the same basic perspective, you can begin to appreciate why sharp disagreements arise among economists. How long do the states of rest remain unchanged? Where should strict rules be set, and who is best at setting them? How much does the assumption of rational self-interest allow for charity, personal caring, and giving back to society?

Regardless of individual differences, the fundamental recognition that equilibrium states include both costs and benefits, that self-interest individuals maximize in any setting, and that saying NO is just as important as saying YES in a scarce world have carried the economics profession a long way. Like music, modern economics requires first learning the rules. The creations come later.

The Remaining Chapters

Chapter Two begins with a discussion of Adam Smith's life and ideas. The distinction between microeconomics and macroeconomics is drawn, and individual-group conflicts are highlighted. Three alerts to the reasoning of modern economics are also provided.

Chapter Three takes up the basics of a purely-competitive market. Alfred Marshall's blades of demand and supply are shown to be able to predict with 100% certainty what will happen under various conditions including price controls by the government. Externalities, monopoly power, and useful knowledge flows in the marketplace are then introduced. For those wishing practical applications, the appendices provide four examples of competitive market analyses.

Chapter Four turns to pricing solutions proposed by modern microeconomic thought. Formal equilibrium pricing models are presented for pure (perfect) competition, monopolistic competition, oligopoly, pure nondiscriminating monopoly, and price discrimination by degrees. The ideas are extended to address skimming, penetration pricing, multiproduct pricing including loss leaders, and the transfer price of inputs within a firm.

Chapter Five provides the technical transition from microeconomic thinking to macroeconomics. The general history of money is examined first, followed by a monetary history of the U.S. Next, concepts of national product and national income are laid out. Say's Law and the inherent stability of capitalism at full employment are then confronted. The chapter ends with the valuable macro framework of the Equation of Exchange.

Chapter Six jumps into the macroeconomic thicket by summarizing ten schools of thought from left to right. It highlights the shifting nature of big time macro debates and the major players involved. Personal beliefs and background are influential here, and nine outlook differences are distinguished.

Finally, Chapter Seven dives into the shark-infested waters of forecasting the U.S. economy over the next ten years. As well as macro theory, demographic patterns and the economic performance of the U.S. president administrations since World War II are reviewed before actual forecasts are given. As you will see, I'm optimistic about the future of the U.S. But what would you expect from a 52 year-old baby-boomer with a 6 year-old son!

How selfish so ever man be supposed,
there are evidently some principles in his nature,
which interest him in the fortune of others,
and render their happiness necessary to him,
though he derives nothing from it
except the pleasure of seeing it.
—*Adam Smith*

It is not from the benevolence of the butcher, the
brewer, or the baker, that we expect our dinner,
but from their regard to their own interest.
—*Adam Smith*

CHAPTER TWO

ADAM SMITH, MICRO VERSUS MACRO, AND ALERTS TO MODERN ECONOMIC THOUGHT

Treatises dealing with the overall economy and specific solutions to particular economic problems existed long before Adam Smith's *An Inquiry into the Nature and Causes of the Wealth of Nations* appeared in 1776. For example, a significant part of the *Wealth of Nations* is devoted to criticizing the ideas of Mercantilism, the prevailing economic philosophy that first arose in the mid-16th century.

Nevertheless, Smith ushered in modern economic thought in large part because he explored many of the same problems that societies confront today. His answers to these problems are based on the fundamental assumption that nations are comprised of *rational individuals* constantly trying to maximize wealth in light of social, economic, and governmental constraints.

A biographical sketch of Smith's life begins the next section, followed by a list of key ideas from the *Wealth of Nations*.

Microeconomics is then distinguished from macroeconomics, and concepts stressing the potential conflict between individual maximization and group objectives are summarized. Key alerts about the word "free" in modern economic thought, the overwhelming importance of prevailing social attitudes, and the paradoxical nature of economic thought conclude the discussions.

Adam Smith and Key Ideas from the Wealth of Nations

Adam Smith enjoyed an amazingly charmed life as a young man, worldly philosopher, and government official.

Born on June 5, 1723 in Kirkcaldy, Fifeshire, Scotland, to a deeply revered mother, who was widowed by the time of his birth, Smith was kidnapped by gypsies as a young boy. He was a frail child, entered Glasgow College at 14, and was strongly influenced by Francis Hutcheson, earning a master of arts degree in three years. From 1740 to 1746, he attended Balliol College, Oxford, which he deemed an educational disaster because of the poor quality of teaching (doesn't this sound familiar!). In 1748, he began giving popular public lectures in Edinburgh on subjects ranging from rhetoric to jurisprudence.

In 1751 Smith was elected to the professorship of logic by the faculty at Glasgow College, and the next year was promoted to Professor of Moral Philosophy. His courses included lectures about natural theology, ethics, justice, and "expediency" (riches, power, and prosperity). At this time he also met frequently with a discussion group of Glasgow merchants, bankers, and manufacturers. *The Theory of Moral Sentiments* appeared in 1759. Here Smith argued that humans are governed by "sentiments" (passions, prosperities, affections, feelings) that are endowed by God. People sympathize (have shared moral sentiments) with each other, which allows them to understand other viewpoints and determine what is proper. Smith concludes that individuals ought to undertake socially-productive, moral lives. (The first quote of this chapter is from *The Theory of Moral Sentiments*).

The fame Smith attracted from this work led to an invitation to travel as a tutor for the young Scottish duke of Buccleuch. In France from 1763 to 1766, this provided Smith access to leading intellectuals of the day. Upon return to England in 1766, he advised the duke's stepfather, Charles Townshend, who subsequently endowed Smith with a generous pension for life in 1767.

An Inquiry into the Nature and Causes of the Wealth of Nations was begun at this time. It finally appeared in 1776, three months before the American Revolution, and became an immediate best seller. Benjamin Franklin and Thomas Jefferson read drafts while in Europe. (The second quote of this chapter is perhaps the most famous one from the *Wealth of Nations*).

Smith served as Commissioner of Customs and Salt Duties of Scotland in Edinburgh from 1778 to the end of his life. However, he did *not* instigate his own free-trade proposals. Appointed the Lord Rector of Glasgow College in 1787, Smith died a bachelor on July 17, 1790, at age sixty-seven when life expectancy was 35. He asked that his unfinished manuscript be destroyed a week before his death due to his humble wish not to leave his ideas incomplete and imperfect.

Everything considered, Adam Smith was, as Nobel laureate George Stigler concluded, "As great as economist as who has ever lived." Joseph Schumpeter, from the perspective of one of the most prolific economic historians of the 20th century, added that, "From about 1790 on, Smith became the teacher not of the beginner or the public but of the profession, especially the professors."

Before considering the ideas of the *Wealth of Nations*, please keep two points in mind. First, while Smith is regarded as a secular humanist searching for economic truths as distinguished from religious musings, he did not see his ideas as being inconsistent with a good, Christian life. Along the lines of Calvin, the *Wealth of Nations* argues that economic freedoms are "natural rights" necessary for the dignity of humankind.

Second, Smith was responding to Mercantilism, the dominant economic philosophy of his day. The Mercantilists looked at the rising power of Spain in the mid-1500's and concluded that the wealth of a nation is the gold and silver – the specie – held in its state's coffers. Therefore, a country should strive for a "favorable balance of trade", in which it exports more than it imports, so that specie flows into state coffers from other countries. Restraints on trade through tariffs and import quotas are necessary, as are monopolies-of-the-crown (single producers licensed by the state to monitor trade more closely). In sum, people's lives need to be strongly regulated by the crown.

The immediate and obvious flaw with Mercantilism in improving overall welfare in the world is that not all countries can simultaneously export more than they import. But Smith goes far deeper in his criticisms. Remember Smith was delving into both the *nature* and the *causes* of a nation's wealth. The key ideas found in the *Wealth of Nations'* are:

- **Money (gold and silver) is not the wealth of a nation.** Money only represents a claim on wealth. If money is wealth, countries could simply print large quantities of it to raise living standards. Instead, *the true wealth of a nation is measured by the goods and services it produces and consumes*, an idea universally accepted in modern economics.
- **The value of a good is determined by the labor embodied in it**. In addressing the water-diamond para-

dox (which asks why water, essential for life, has a low value or price, and conversely why diamonds have a high value), Smith emphasized a labor theory of value – a cost of production theory of value. Water takes less labor to acquire than diamonds. The labor theory of value is a flaw in Smith's reasoning according to contemporary economics. Value is determined by the interaction between demand and supply, not just the cost of production as the *Wealth of Nations* proposes. Nonetheless, the labor theory embodies the individualistic, micro perspective of Smith.

- **A major cause of the wealth of a nation is division and specialization of labor.** Smith gave a famous example of ladies hat pins: a single worker without machines can't make more than 20 pins a day; but ten people, dividing tasks up and working with specialized equipment, can produce 48,000 a day. Economists since have readily agreed that division and specialization enhances productivity and raises living standards.

- **A major cause of the wealth of nations is capital formation (saving and investing).** Book II of the *Wealth of Nations* explores the necessity of capital formation to achieve economic growth, making distinctions between gross and net investment, fixed (buildings, machinery) and circulating (inventories) capital, and the idea of human capital (labeled "acquired and useful abilities"). Economists since have agreed that accumulation of capital enhances labor productivity and is necessary for economic progress.

- **Free trade—no tariffs and quotas—increases the wealth of a nation.** VOLUNTARY EXCHANGE BENEFITS BOTH PARTIES. Furthermore, free trade creates larger markets and therefore allows greater division of labor (what good is it to produce 48,000 hat pins if they cannot all be traded for goods?). Free trade of legal goods always benefits consumers because they have more choices, and typically at lower prices, than without trade. Tariffs and quotas are harmful restraints. Free trade is a WIN-WIN situation to use current-day terminology.

- **A nation's institutional structures have to be set up properly for market forces to flourish.** In particular, the government must protect its citizens from external threats through national defense, must administer justice through fair court and police systems, and must provide public goods like roads, canals, and bridges to enhance goods and services flowing from the point of production to the point of consumption.

- **Money supply and credit growth must be thoughtfully regulated.** Fairly strict banking regulations are mandatory in order to maintain the security necessary to foster growth. To prevent banks from over-issuing paper money, loans must be restricted to real bills of credit. With a gold standard in place, banks have the freedom to issue only loans based upon "a *real bill* of exchange drawn by a real creditor upon a real debtor, and which as soon as it becomes due, is really paid by the debtor." These ideas will be expanded in later chapters. The basic theme remains that excessive creation of money and "free banking" is bad for an economy.

- **Individual greed is channeled by "an invisible hand" into societal welfare.** Competition prevents chaos in the economy. This is perhaps the single most important idea in the *Wealth of Nations*. Individual desire for happiness, even outright greed, will lead to the betterment of society if the proper institutions are in place. The inborn propensity to pursue one's own self-interest can maximize *both* individual and national income. To quote Smith, "By pursuing his own interest he frequently promotes that of the society more effectually than when he really intends to promote it." Life is truly paradoxical in this regard.

Microeconomics, Macroeconomics, and Constant Conflict between the Individual and the Group

Smith and subsequent 19th century economists did not make a sharp distinction between "micro" and "macro" economics. The break occurred, instead, in the 1930's when the rationality of individual households and markets appeared to be in conflict with the ability of free-market economies to maintain full employment.

Microeconomics, like a microscope, focuses on small parts of the economy through intense magnification. The behavior of rational individuals (households) and profit-maximizing firms is formulated with precise logic. Individual markets or industries are modeled in a partial equilibrium setting in which a host of other variables (prices of related goods, income, expectations, tastes) are held constant. This is done through the assumption of *ceteris paribus*, which is Latin for "everything else the same." Please keep this assumption in mind—it is a critical feature of every microeconomic model ever constructed.

Microeconomists are similar to chemists or physicists running laboratory experiments. Various elements, such as temperature, atmospheric pressure, humidity, tastes, and other prices are held the same in order to discover or reconfirm scientific laws that hold under the stated conditions. The focus is on *market-specific* analysis to explain and predict various outcomes. We are going tree to tree. The entire forest is another story.

Macroeconomics gives the broader picture. The perspective is the entire economy, not individual households, firms, or markets. Rather than the price and output of a single firm or industry, macroeconomists are interested in overall prices and total output for an economy. Macroeconomists often rely upon general equilibrium instead of partial (single-market) equilibrium. *Aggregate* demand/supply analysis is used to visualize economic adjustments and shocks to the system.

Chapter 2

The existence of *micro* rationality in the broader *macro* setting creates one of the most fundamental puzzles of life. What is true at the individual level may not be true at the group level. Rational, self-maximizing individuals, when thrown together into a group context, can do crazy things that reduce overall utility or profits. Here is a list of individual-group conflicts common in the economic literature:

- **The fallacy of composition.** Just because it is rational for one person to stand at a football game to see better, it doesn't mean everyone should stand to see better. What is true for the individual is not necessarily true for the group.
- **Prisoners' Dilemma.** Two people rob a bank, make a clean getaway, and dispose of the cash. The police pick them up on possible parole violations knowing that they committed the robbery. If neither prisoner confesses, each gets a one-year sentence for parole violations. If one confesses and one doesn't, the first goes free and the other spends ten years in jail. And if both confess, both get seven years in jail. Naturally the first thing the police do is separate the prisoners. Now do the prisoners keep quiet or confess — what a dilemma! The *best* group answer for the prisoners is that neither confesses — will this be the *individual* response?
- **Tragedy of the commons.** Villages in merry old England in the Middle Ages had common grazing land for all citizens to feed their livestock. There was some optimal number of animals from a group perspective that maintains the commons in the long run. But individuals do not have a strong incentive to restrict the number of their animals. The problem is similar for fishing in the sea or polluting the environment. The tragedy of destroying the commons occurs whenever property rights are not carefully defined.
- **The inevitable collapse of cartels.** A cartel is a group of firms trying to act like a monopoly, typically to raise price. Yet to raise price they must restrict output and

assign quotas to individual producers. Once the quotas are in a place, producers have excess capacity and thus have a strong incentive to cut price to try to increase sales significantly. Free-market economists believe that this inevitably causes cartels to collapse even in the absence of government intervention.

- **The paradox of majority voting.** The idea can be traced to Smith's contemporary Marquis de Condorcet and is often linked in economic literature to Nobel laureate Kenneth Arrow. Just because three individuals are rational in their preferences among three choices and thereby can order them transitively—meaning, if choice A is preferred to B, and B to C, then A is preferred to C—it does not mean that group voting will exhibit rational behavior.

For example, consider the following behavior among three people who have transitive preferences for three alternative choices: A, B, and C. For Mrs. White: A is preferred to B, B is preferred to C, so A is preferred to C. For Ms. Brown: B is preferred to C, C is preferred to A, so B is preferred to A. For Mr. Black: C is preferred to A, A is preferred to B, so C is preferred to B. If we compare A and B, Mrs. White and Mr. Black prefer A to B while Ms. Brown does not, meaning A is preferred to B by 2 to 1. If we compare B to C, Mrs. White and Ms. Brown prefer B to C while Mr. Black does not, meaning B is preferred to C by 2 to 1. By group transitivity A should then be preferred to C. Yet in actual voting Ms. Brown and Mr. Black prefer C to A and Mrs. White doesn't, meaning C is preferred to A by 2 to 1! The conclusion is startling: rational individual preferences do not necessarily imply rational group outcomes in a democratic voting environment.

- **Paradox of thrift.** This idea, often tied to Keynesian economics, rejects the benefits of saving at certain times. As households save more of their income when they anticipate a downturn in the economy, this is bad for society as a whole. Less spending means less production, which means lower employment levels and income. Indeed, attempts to save more may actually create less total saving than what households anticipated!

- **Moral hazards.** Various rules and regulations arise that lead large numbers of individuals to undertake very risky behavior to themselves or their institutions that in turn, becomes detrimental to society. For example, in the case of the savings and loan industry in the 1980's, when the government insured depositors from losses on their accounts, individual financial institutions adopted riskier and riskier investments — assumed greater moral hazards — in search of greater profit. The end-result was that the entire financial system was put in more jeopardy.

Each of these conflicts situations clearly demonstrate that, as rational individuals seek to maximize utility, total profits, or their economic rents, mob and herd mentalities can run amok. Microeconomists can never forget this element of life.

Three Additional Alerts to Modern Economic Thought

Beyond the problems associated with distinguishing between rational, individual actions versus group outcomes, a far greater understanding of modern economics thought is achieved if three other alerts are kept firmly in mind as well.

Free: The Most Dangerous Word in Economics and Perhaps the Entire English Language

According to *Webster's New World Dictionary*, over twenty different meanings are listed for the word "free". The range from "not confined to the usual rules or patterns" to "not restricted by anything except its own limitations or nature" to "generous; liberal; lavish" to "open to all, especially without restrictions as to trade". What is missing here is that in modern economic terms, FREE DOES NOT MEAN FREE.

The most recognized economic phrase by the general public today is, "There is no such thing as a free lunch". In other words, even if the money price of a lunch is zero, the time to eat the meal has value and could be spent elsewhere. So a lunch can never be "free". Likewise, "free" trade means the lack of tariffs, quotas, and other restrictive government regulations; it does not mean the unrestricted "freedom" to conduct piracy, physical threats, bribery, or cheating on agreements. A "free" market is defined by ease of entry and exit, lack of price controls, and the general opportunity to be rewarded; it does not mean the right to set your own rules and fix prices with competitors.

Constraints are always present under conditions of scarcity. FREE MEANS THAT YOU MUST ALWAYS BE PREPARED TO SAY NO. Responsibility demands it. Personal freedom has tremendously high costs. So whenever you hear something is free, be prepared to duck your head and climb into a bunker.

Economic Theories Are Argued Against the Backdrop of Contemporary Life

No social argument is ever free of its immediate environment. Accordingly, economic theories are always argued against the backdrop of current issues. For example, the dominance of manufacturing in Western economies at the end of the 19th century led economists to formulate "natural laws" concerning returns to labor and to capital and the "true nature" of business cycles. Similarly the Great Depression gave birth to Keynesian economics, with its spirited defense of government intervention and its "truths" about aggregate demand. Then the lengthy economic expansion since the early 1980's have led some economists to ask if the new era of global capitalism is now the "new paradigm", with Keynesian economics viewed as only a minor subpiece.

Such influences of contemporary issues on economic thought are inevitable. Each new generation of economists believes that it knows much more than previous generations of economists because of the increasing store of human knowledge from which to draw. But always remember that economics is the only discipline where two people can win Nobel prizes for saying exactly opposite things.

Paradoxes Left and Right

When I first started teaching economics, I told students that most of economics is just plain common sense. What a naive viewpoint. Common sense – or perhaps better yet, common belief – can lead you widely astray in modern economic thought. There are too many paradoxes, ironies, and incongruities that require more than common sense or personal feelings to understand. We have already seen that individual greed can be highly beneficial for society through the invisible hand or that basic products can have a low value (price) even though they are needed for survival. Rational prisoners may cause themselves too much time in jail, and democracies of rational voters with transitive preferences may end up with non-rational group results.

Subsequent chapters consider ideas that require more than common sense to understand. Debates about the minimum wage, price restrictions, government controls on the flows of knowledge, the demand for children, and ticket scalping all require going beyond heartfelt beliefs in order to sort out truth from fantasy. Paradoxes abound, and good intentions do not always mean good results.

CHAPTER THREE

THE GLORIOUS INSIGHTS OF
FREE-MARKET MICROECONOMIC THOUGHT

Microeconomic thinking is a carefully constructed jigsaw puzzle. From the time of Adam Smith through the emergence of Marshallian thought at the end of the 19th century, the foundation pieces were put in place.

Today, microeconomists have the ability to explain how and why various market situations have occurred and how others will unfold. Firm and household behavior are modeled for all kinds of profit and nonprofit settings. The clear-cut objective is to improve the welfare (happiness, satisfaction, or utility) of individuals and groups using sound, logical reasoning.

In terms of gender, race, and religious differences, micro-economists are well-aware that certain groups of people act differently than others due to the special social constraints surrounding their lives. But free-market reasoning is driven by the idea that all rational people are *rent seekers*: everyone wants rewards above and beyond "normal". Accordingly, *all* rational individuals respond to basic economic laws in essentially the same manner.

Of course, economic models can be constructed on racial discrimination, differentials in wage rates between the sexes, and other personal traits. However, the following micro analysis sets aside gender, race, and religious differences. Individual firms and households are treated in light of skills, motivation, cleverness, honesty, and the desire to innovate, NOT PHYSICAL APPEARANCE. Competitive markets reward entrepreneurial skills and qualities. The fundamental question to a free-market economist is: Who can get the job done optimally with the best mix of price and quality for the consumer?

Inefficient mistakes and errors can certainly arise. However, the efficiency of the free market process in total is overwhelming. Free markets generate a stunning array of goods and services for consumers in the U.S. And this is done through the innovation and hard work of individuals. As General George S. Patton recognized, "Never tell people *how* to do things. Tell them *what* to do and they will surprise you with their ingenuity."

The next section highlights of Alfred Marshall's principles of free-market microeconomic thought. These include marginalism-equimarginalism, the Law of Opportunity Cost, the Law of Diminishing Physical Returns plus related per-unit costs, and the determination of equilibrium price and quantity through the inter-action of demand and supply curves. Extensions to Marshall's basic market reasoning follow: externalities and the Coase Theorem, the nature of business cycles in light of Joseph Schumpeter's "creative destruction", and the useful flow of knowledge as seen by F.A. Hayek. These arguments greatly enhance our appreciation of how the competitive marketplace functions day-to-day.

Four real-world applications of neoclassical micro theory are found in the appendices. The first looks at road-and-driving markets. These markets clearly require very selective regulations—the issue is where the constraints (lines) must be drawn. The second analyzes the allocation of faculty offices in the ASU College of Business through various schemes, including sealed bids. The third ventures into ticket scalping, an emotional issue for many consumers today. Last comes the microeconomic model household fertility decisions by Nobel laureate Gary Becker and fellow Chicago-Columbia (new home) economists, demonstrating the degree to which core micro theory can be carried into very personal decisions. It is here we encounter the infamous rotten-kid theorem, one of the more clever insights in modern microeconomic thought.

Alfred Marshall and the Basic Laws of Microeconomics

Alfred Marshall, like Adam Smith, led a very productive, scholarly life.

Born on July 26, 1842 to a highly-religious, Evangelical, Victorian father who was a cashier at the Bank of England, Marshall was slated by his father to go to Oxford to become an Anglican minister. Instead he began the study of mathematics at St. John's College, Cambridge in 1869 through the help of a kindly uncle. He was a top student and ultimately taught mathematics at Cambridge.

In 1868 Marshall traveled to Germany, where he was influenced by noted philosophers and economists. He served as a fellow and lecturer in moral science at Cambridge from 1868 to 1877, becoming involved in economics because of his deep concern for the social problems of the poor. He also visited the United States in 1875 and was strongly influenced by its frontier, capitalistic spirit.

When he married Mary Paley, a former pupil, in 1877, Marshall was forced to give up his fellowship at Cambridge because of university restrictions. He became a professor of political economy at University College, Bristol for five years and published *The Economics of Industry* in 1879. Spending 1881-1882 in Italy due to ill health, he then served as lecturer in political economy at Balliol College, Oxford from 1883-1885. He finally returned in 1885 to Cambridge when the marriage restrictions were lifted.

The period from 1885 to 1908 was highly productive. His *Principles of Economics* appeared in 1890, plus he authored a number of important government commissions during this period. He fought effectively in convincing the Cambridge faculty that economics (as opposed to political economy) was truly a science with verifiable laws just like physics and chemistry, thus justifying its status as a university subject. Some of the top economists of the day were his students, including Frances Y. Edgeworth, Cecil A. Pigou, and John M. Keynes (Marshall was a friend and colleague of Keynes' father, John Neville Keynes, also a faculty member at Cambridge).

In 1908, Marshall retired from his chair at Cambridge due to his perceptions of failing health. He still managed to write *Industry and Trade* in 1919, which detailed the various forms of Western capitalism at the beginning of the twentieth century. Marshall struggled to turn out *Money, Credit, and Commerce* in 1923, and he finally died on July 13, 1924.

Marshall is now acknowledged as the founder of the Cambridge School, a leading light in British economics for decades, the originator of modern neoclassical microeconomic reasoning, and one of the major figures responsible for the scientific professionalism of modern economics.

Marginalism and Equimarginalism

Microeconomists love the word *marginal*. The *marginal unit* is either the next unit to be consumed (produced) or the last unit to be consumed. To use a common analogy, it can be the straw that breaks the camel's back. In microeconomics, the *marginal costs* (MC) of an item are the added costs (beyond those already incurred) of producing one more unit. Similarly, the *marginal revenue* (MR) of an item is the added revenue generated by selling one more unit. A profit-maximizing firm constantly compares marginal costs to marginal revenue as it seeks to maximize total profits. Whenever MR>MC, total profits are expanding. Accordingly, the firm works to the point where

MR=MC, and it is at this level of production is where total profits are their greatest.

You may have heard about "being at the margin" – being just at the edge. There are "marginal" businesses, "marginal" pieces of land, and "marginal" levels of income. Many individuals don't like marginal in this survival sense. However, a rational decision-maker always uses the marginalist perspective when addressing life's problems. To be a RATIONAL MARGINALIST means the following:

- **Setting an overall objective.** Typically, the objective is total utility maximization for individuals or total profit maximization for firms.
- **Recognizing binding constraints, especially in terms of time.** Marshall emphasized different time horizons, each involving different decision-making constraints. The *short run* is the time period in which technology – the state of knowledge – is fixed, and so is at least one factor of production. Fixed in this context means that it is too costly to vary quickly, and typically plant/equipment is the fixed factor in the short run. All ongoing economic activity takes place either in the short run or in the extreme short-run (Marshall's so-called *market period* in which all factors of production are fixed). The *long run* is the time period in which technology is fixed, but all factors of production are variable. It is the blueprint or planning stage in which the plant size for future operation in the short run is chosen. The *very long run* is the time period in which the basic state of knowledge about production is changing, making old plants obsolete. Paradoxically, it can be quite brief in highly innovative industries. The rational decision maker readily recognizes the differences between the three time horizons and knows just what is variable and what is fixed at any moment. In other words, the rational decision-maker knows the binding constraints.

- **To improve totals, the marginalist thinks on a per-unit basis.** The marginalist constantly contemplates making small, incremental changes in consumption or production in order to improve on total utility or total profits.
- **To achieve the very best results, the marginalist must be an EQUIMARGINALIST.** To maximize total profits, a firm must reach the point where marginal revenue equals marginal costs. If the additional revenue from the next or last unit sold is greater than the additional cost, the firm expands sales, and continues to do so until equality between the two is reached. Only by equating marginal values—going to the point where marginal revenue equals marginal costs— does a decision-maker achieve optimal total profits.

Thus, an equimarginalist is constantly thinking about "being at the margin" in the sense of being pushed to some limit. At the same time, an equimarginalist is normally not running a "marginal" business or being a "marginal" employee. Instead, true equimarginalists have maximized themselves away from marginal existences!

The Law of Opportunity Cost, Plus the Notion of Sunk Cost

Most people are familiar with the notion of *opportunity cost.* Let's be precise. *Opportunity cost is defined as the full value of the best alternative given up for the one you have chosen.* Three ideas are key in this definition.

First, there are always alternatives with any decision or with using any resource. *Always, always, always!* The opportunity cost of any choice is then the *best* of these alternatives foregone in terms of profit or utility.

Second, the definition emphasizes *full* value. It does not say the difference between the actual choice and best alternative. OPPORTUNITY COST IS NEVER ZERO because something of value is always being foregone. Indeed, this is the Law of Opportunity Cost. It's the same as saying that there are never free lunches, that you can't have your cake (keep it on the plate) and eat it too, or that you can't be in two places at once. You simply cannot do everything you want to.

Nothing causes me to cringe more than hearing supposedly intelligent individuals, particularly professionally-trained economists, who proclaim that the opportunity cost of some choice is zero. What they are really saying is either that the best alternative is so incredibly costly that they have ruled it out, or that they can think of no conceivable alternative at the moment. Be extremely wary of anyone who says some opportunity cost is zero—they don't know what they're talking about.

The final point to remember about opportunity cost is that, from the individual's perspective, "viable" alternatives are always self-defined. Only you know if you are in your "best" alternative at any moment and if you have made the "best" choices up to that point. The opportunity cost of any personal decision is highly subjective. For some people, this is scary. They constantly fret about past decisions or wonder why they continually confront poor alternatives. For others, the attitude is quite different. They would not trade places with any other person either present or past. They readily recognize that everyone has significant opportunity costs in life, but they understand theirs better than anybody else's. In fact, some people would not even want to relive a minute of their life because they are grounded in the present: they did the best they could at the time and have learned from past mistakes.

Closely involved in the consideration of opportunity cost is the idea of *sunk costs*: those outlays that are essentially non-recoverable at this moment (like an oil well buried in the ground). These costs can cloud thinking when calculating opportunity cost. You are operating at the margin, and just because you have invested a tremendous amount of time or money on some project doesn't mean you should necessarily be able to recover it. Recovering past losses may be impossible, and truly sunk costs must pushed aside when calculating present opportunity cost. Crying over spilled milk is a waste of both milk and tears.

Chapter 3

The Law of Diminishing Physical Returns and Related Per-Unit Costs

"The world can't be fed from a flowerpot." This simple expression is just another way of stating the Law of Diminishing Physical Returns. The emphasis is on the physical world, physical boundaries, and physical constraints.

The Law of Diminishing Returns is a short-run concept to use Marshall's terminology. Technology, the state of knowledge about how to produce, is held constant. So is *at least* one factor of production. Then the Law of Diminishing Returns indicates how total, average, and marginal products change as variable factors are added to the fixed factor. The law indicates that all three products must eventually diminish (begin to decline).

Let's consider the simple situation where workers are being added to a fixed plant. A *plant* in microeconomics is any physical unit of production and may be a department store, a factory, an acre of land, a coalmine, a bulldozer, or a nuclear reactor. Figure 3.1 demonstrates the Law of Diminishing Physical Returns for a department store. For those readers who hate graphs, just remember that a picture can really be worth a thousand words. Moreover, you can dazzle friends at cocktail parties with a quick economic sketch.

Adding the first worker means that person must do everything from waiting on customers to ringing up sales to gift wrapping to accepting returned items. A second worker creates division and specialization effects. Various tasks can be separated and the two workers become more specialized. This may continue for quite some time as additional workers are added to the department store, especially if it is a "big" store. *Total output* increases at an increasing rate up to point A (L_A workers), and so does both the output per worker (*average product*) and the output relative to the previous worker (*marginal product*).

However, sooner-or-later the division and specialization effects are exhausted, so the marginal output of each additional worker begins to diminish after point A. This doesn't mean that each additional worker has immediately stopped adding to total output. Average product continues to increase beyond A. *What it does mean is that each additional worker is no longer adding as much as the previous worker,* so marginal product must begin to fall. It is at point A that the Law of Diminishing Physical returns begins to take hold. Point B (L_B workers) is where average product begins to decline.

Figure 3.1: The Law of Diminishing Physical Returns

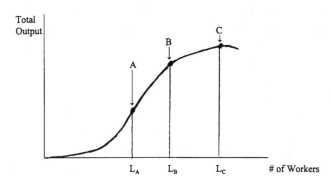

Of course, if too many workers are added to the store, they crowd out customers. Marginal product becomes negative, and total product diminishes after point C. But remember, in Marshallian microeconomics, the Law of Diminishing Physical Returns sets in where the *marginal product* of the variable factor begins to fall, not where the *total product* begins to fall.

The Law of Diminishing Physical Returns is the basis for Thomas Malthus' claims that masses of humanity will be doomed to subsistence levels of living in the long run even with division and specialization effects present. The earth is assumed fixed, and since advances in technology cannot possibly keep pace with population growth due to the "passion between the sexes", the marginal product of labor will be pushed downward to subsistence levels for the masses. The Iron Law of Wages (not only a law, but one cast in iron!) indicates the consequences of physical constraints in driving down living conditions the absence of improvements in technology and greater capital formulation.

The shape of our total output curve is S-shaped, and S-shaped curves abound in the current decision-making literature on new products and markets. At first things take off slowly. But then the product/idea catches on, and it's like a rocket flight to the moon for a while. But eventually frictions, drags, depreciation, or whatever stop the exponential take-off, and the new products or markets settle into the mature stage. The critical point here is that as long as something variable is being added to something fixed, laws of atrophy and attribution must occur in our universe.

Let's now visualize short-run per unit cost curves for S-curve situations. Such cost curves are quite commonplace, and an understanding enhances personal choices and sets up the pricing discussions in the next chapter.

We assume that labor and capital, our two inputs, are bought in competitive markets. Thus wages (W) and the price of capital (C) are fixed. We continue to assume variable labor (L) is being added to a given plant (K). Accordingly, there are average fixed costs (AFC), average variable costs (AVC), average costs (AC), and marginal costs (MC) in the short run that change in relation to output (Q).

In this example *average fixed costs* (AFC) equal $\frac{\overline{K} \cdot \overline{C}}{Q}$. The numerator (total fixed costs) is a constant, thus as more output is produced, AFC must fall continuously. This is also called the "spreading overhead". *Average variable costs* (AVC) equal $\frac{L \cdot \overline{W}}{Q}$. At first AVC fall as the average product of labor (Q/L) rises due to division and specialization effects combined with each additional worker receiving the same wage. Then the Law of Diminishing Physical Returns begins to drive down the average product of labor, so AVC must turn up.

Similarly, marginal costs (MC) are the change in total costs when one more unit of output is produced. Using the Greek letter "Δ" to signify change, in our example MC equal

$$\Delta(\overline{W} \bullet L + \overline{C} \bullet \overline{K})/\Delta Q = \Delta(\overline{W} \bullet L)/\Delta Q = \overline{W}(\Delta L/\Delta Q)$$

As the marginal product of labor (ΔQ/ΔL) goes up, MC fall. Once the Law of Diminishing Physical Returns in, MC begin to rise. Point A in Figure 3.2 corresponds to point A in Figure 3.1, and likewise for the points B and C in the two figures.

Figure 3.2 Per Unit Cost Curves in the Short Run

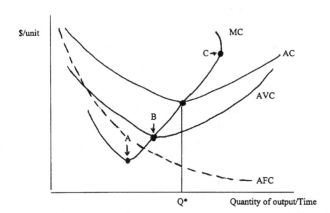

Average costs (AC) equal AFC + AVC. Therefore, they start out high and descend due to spreading overhead and division and specification effects. AC continue to fall even after AVC turn upward as the spreading of overhead offsets diminishing physical returns. However, AC must reach a minimum point (Q*). This represents the most efficient point of production under existing technology. Only here do MC=AC. After Q*, AC rise sharply and come closer and closer to AVC as overhead is spread over many units of output.

Price Determination Through Demand and Supply

Adam Smith adopted a labor theory of value, as did Malthus, Marx, and other economists through the first two-thirds of the 19th century. In the 1870's, Austrian economists at the University of Vienna, led by Carl Menger, and English economists, led by Stanley Jevons, countered with a utility theory of value. They based their arguments on *utils*— jolts of joy— in individuals' minds. Their answer to the water-diamond paradox is that water has a low price because the marginal utility of the last unit consumed is minimal, even though total utility is great, whereas diamonds have a high price because the marginal utility of the last unit consumed is significant, even though total utility is far less than water.

Marshall, the great synthesizer, brought these opposing views together in 1890. He made price determination a two-pronged phenomenon, making the analogy to blades of a scissors. It involves both the elements of personal desire and the constraints of the physical world. We begin with the Law of Demand.

(1) The Law of Demand!

The Law of Demand is where Marshall deserves the most acclaim for moving economics to the level of a science. The Law of Opportunity Cost and the Law of Diminishing Physical Returns were well-understood before Marshall. In order to convince the hard-core physical scientists at Cambridge that economics was indeed a science, he needed a unique law that was just as universal as the basic laws of motion or chemical interactions.

The Law of Demand says that consumers *desire* to purchase *more* of a good as its relative price *falls*, and *less* as its relative price *rises*, in a given time period, *ceteris paribus*. First and foremost, this law does not deny that a variety of factors affect the final demand of any good or service. Household incomes, prices of related products, the demographic make-up of the buying population, expectations of the future, and individual preferences are all important. But the Law of Demand focuses on the RELATIVE PRICE of the good or service. All other factors are held constant in this controlled experiment.

The relative price of any good or service consists of two elements: (1) its money or market price, and (2) the opportunity cost of time involved in its acquisition and final consumption. If the price for some good falls *relative* to the prices of other goods and services, with everything else constant, consumers in total will want more in a given time period. That's why it's a "good" rather than a "bad". A typical market demand curve (naturally drawn as a straight line) is seen in Figure 3.3. This market demand curve is the summation of all individual demand curves.

The Law of Demand doesn't mean that each and every consumer will buy more as relative price falls, only that overall there is be a greater desire to purchase the item. Also, it doesn't mean that every fall in money price will increase the actual quantity purchased. The time component of price may be rising or other factors may be changing to offset falls in money price. What the Law of Demand makes crystal clear is that price always affect purchase in a predictable manner under *ceteris paribus* conditions.

Figure 3.3: The Market For a Final Good or Service

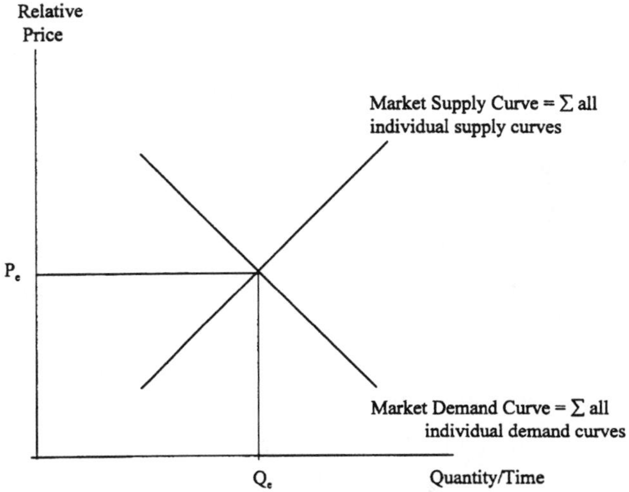

(2) The Law of Supply?

Economic discussions often make reference to the "laws of demand and supply". Is there a Law of Supply that is just as universal as the Law of Demand? Not quite.

The standard Law of Supply states that firms in total *desire* to sell *more* output in a given time period as the relative price *increases, ceteris paribus.* In other words, the market supply curve, as seen in Figure 3.3, is upward sloping to the right. Again, everything else is held constant, including money wages, technology, prices of related goods, number of firms, and expectations. The market supply curve is the summation of all individual firms' supply curves (the individual marginal cost curves in Figure 3.2).

Generally, a firm's total profits will be greater as more output is sold. If prices for the firm's output are increasing while wages and capital costs are constant, total profits will increase for an extended range of output. Hypothetically, market supply curves can eventually bend back (slope upward to the left) when too many workers are added causing total output to actually diminish. Since no rational firm operates in this manner, constant-wage situations are consistent with an upward-to-the-right sloping market supply curves for manufactured products, department stores, and other outputs made in plants.

Turning to supply curves for labor effort, rising wage rates will cause the number of worked hours and productive effort to increase only up to a point. Then leisure desires set in, and further increases in wages lead to less work time. The supply curve of labor, showing the relationship between hours worked and relative wages, begins to bend back (slope upward to the left). Such backward-bending labor supply curves can create backward-bending market supply curves, notably in small, labor-intensive industries in which firms choose to produce less as market prices go up significantly.

As for highly technological industries, when innovation is coming rapidly like in the production of computer chips, falling prices are associated with more units supplied rather than less. Such dynamic, innovation-driven supply curves are downward sloping because of the increasing returns. Standard analysis seems wrong. But keep in mind that the *ceteris paribus* assumption is being violated here.

The market analyses that follow assume conventional, upward-sloping-to-the-right supply curves. The more esoteric backward-bending or downward-sloping-to-the-right models are on the edge of Marshallian thought.

(3) The Two Blades of a Scissors—
Demand and Supply Determine Price

Marshall's simple analogy for the necessity of both demand and supply curves to determine price is that they are like two blades of scissors. Just as one blade cannot cut a piece of paper, neither demand alone nor supply alone can determine market price. Figure 3.3 continues to be the most famous picture in all of economics: market demand and supply conditions in a competitive environment.

Let's now be quite precise about the axes in Figure 3.3. On the vertical axis, Marshall put money price. By holding everything else constant, notably the time price, this becomes the relative money price of the good. Price remains on the vertical axis today, even though it is the independent variable in standard discussions, because Marshall first put it there (he assumed quantity rather than price was the independent variable).

On the horizontal axis, Marshall put quantity measured over some time period, (a day, a month, a year). Because both supply and demand are expressed per a given time period, they are *flow* variables. They require a passage of time to measure, as opposed to *stock* variables, ones able to be added up at an instant in time. Demand and supply curves are, in essence, slices of time taken out of a continuously moving motion picture.

The market demand curve shows how much consumers *would like to buy* at each price, not the amount they *actually* buy. Similarly, the market supply curve shows how much producers *would like to sell* at each price, not the amount *actually* sold. What happens next?

Assuming that there are no government-mandated price controls, the market will settle down at equilibrium price P_e and equilibrium quantity Q_e in Figure 3.3. *Equilibrium here is a stable state of rest.* If the relative money price is above P_e, then desired supply (more precisely, desired quantity supplied) is greater than desired demand (more precisely, desired quantity demanded). This causes producers to compete price down to P_e. If the relative money price is below P_e, desired demand is greater than desired supply. Buyers now compete price up to P_e. Only at P_e does desired quantity demanded equal desired quantity supplied.

Are consumers happy with P_e? Maybe and maybe not. Consumers generally want lower prices. Are producers happy with P_e? Maybe and maybe not. Producers generally want higher prices. So who's truly happy? For the most part, only free-market economists who see this as the best way of resolving the thousands and thousands of conflicting desires that operate continuously in any market setting. Market price is beyond the control of politicians or government boards who think they know what's really "right" or "fair".

Competitive markets are driven by the demanders willing to pay the price at which producers are willing to sell. Certainly this has elements of discrimination. From the spending side, it favors people with higher incomes. But remember that conflict is inevitable, and not everybody is going to get what they want. To free-market advocates, the allocation of final goods and services, which is based on who is willing to pay the price, is far better than allocations based on race, gender, religion, or first-come-first-served.

What happens if the government, in its infinite wisdom, decides to implement either a price control or a price support in a competitive market? Figure 3.4 helps show with absolute certainty what will occur.

Figure 3.4: Price Controls by the Government

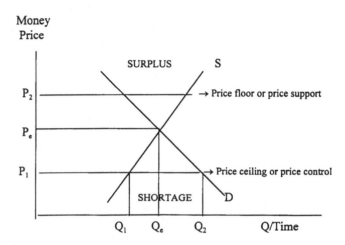

P_e is the price that "clears the market". This means no lines or queues exist for the good. If the federal government decides that this equilibrium price is too high and unfair, it can impose a PRICE CONTROL – set a price ceiling — at P_1. Desired demand, as measured by Q_2, is greater than desired supply, as measured by Q_1. There is an economic SHORTAGE. Not allowing money price to increase to P_e always results in long lines, underground (black-market) transactions, deterioration of quality or service, and most significantly, a problem that just doesn't go away.

For example, rent controls in Berkeley in the late 1960's hurt students rather helped them. They did not readily find cheap, nice apartments near campus as well-intentioned city council members said they would. Instead, potential renters were forced to scan the obituaries for apartment opportunities since people in rent-controlled apartments rarely moved out. Keys, security deposits, and other such related items soared in price. Landlords let apartments deteriorate, and there was little incentive to build new complexes. Students were pushed further away from campus even though the rent controls were supposedly designed to help them.

Similarly, price controls under the Nixon Administration between 1971 and 1974, especially the attempt to keep gasoline prices below free-market levels, led to predictable problems. There were long lines, short tempers, and under-the-table payments, with items like teddy bears being sold at ridiculously high prices in order to gain access to gasoline at the controlled price. Much shorter hours of operation came about quickly, and so did less personal service. Again, the idea was to help the poor get a "necessary" good at a "fair" price. Why should anyone have to pay more for gasoline, an item so critical to the American lifestyle? It seemed too unjust to politicians.

Now, suppose that the government decides that the equilibrium price P_e is too low. It's "unfair" for producers. The government can impose a PRICE SUPPORT—build in a price floor — at P_2 (only the government is capable of getting a floor above a ceiling). At this price, desired supply is greater than desired demand. There is an economic SURPLUS, and here comes true economic insanity. The government, in order to maintain support prices (purchasing-power-parity) for farmers for example, must keep buying up the surplus sugar, milk, or whatever. It then must either store the surplus at high costs, or give it away, or destroy it, or even pay people not to produce it!

The minimum wage represents another example of a price floor. When the government artificially sets a minimum money wage above the free-market level, supposedly to help unskilled workers, unskilled workers will actually be hurt. Employers, faced with a surplus of labor at the government-declared wage, will hire semi-skilled rather than unskilled workers. While the intentions by politicians may be noble, they must face the reality of market laws. What good is it to declare "living" wage if a person can't get a job at that wage?

In sum, the basic nature of a *laissez-faire* markets is that thousands (millions, billions) of individual decisions are coordinated through relative price adjustments with incredible efficiency. Output goes to those willing to pay the price. Certainly not everybody is happy with the market price and quantity. Indeed, a great many people may be quite unhappy. There must always be market rules: some laid down by government, some set by particular boards like those for stock exchanges or futures markets, and some determined by shared moral sentiments. But any government attempts to control price—to try to outguess the forces of demand and supply— result in shortages or surpluses that reduce the wealth of a nation. Marshall's model of a freely competitive market expands upon Smith's invisible hand and lays out a truly wondrous process.

Before we leave free markets, let's consider ideas subsequent to Marshall that have enhanced our understanding of how *laissez-faire* markets actually function. We start with externalities and Ronald Coase's famous theorem, turn to monopolies and Joseph Schumpeter's theory of creative destruction, and finally look at how best to achieve useful knowledge flows according to F. A. Hayek.

Externalities and the Coase Theorem

The word *externality* conveys its economic meaning. This is either a cost or a benefit that is *external* to the market. Someone is either losing utility or gaining utility without someone else taking it directly into account in their market actions. How can such situations be handled?

The classic example of a *cost externality* is pollution. If a steel mill can "freely" dump its waste into the river, then those downstream suffer from the actions. The market price for steel doesn't take this loss of utility directly into account. Little wonder that cost externalities are also called *negative spillover effects*. Another example is when the people next door decide to do something crazy to their house or lawn that reduces the value of other houses on the block. For this reason, cost externalities are also called *negative neighborhood effects*. The tragedy of the commons represents extreme negative neighborhood effects.

A *benefit externality* means that others gain in a positive way from an individual's action, but that the individual is not compensated directly. An example is polio vaccination. If left entirely to personal choice, not everyone will get vaccinated based on internal cost-benefit analysis. Yet everyone benefits if all people are vaccinated, and the spillover effects are extremely positive since the disease is eliminated. Another classic example of a benefit externality is a lighthouse which all ships can see once it is built. There is no incentive for a private firm – the market – to build the lighthouse. Instead, it is a *public good*, where the consumption by one does not preclude consumption by others, making revenues difficult to capture by the private sector.

Externalities are an ongoing feature of life. People either impose spillover costs or create positive neighborhood effects on others as they move through life. What economists want to do as much as possible is to *internalize the externalities into markets* so that the market price reflects all costs and benefits. The standard political suggestions are for the government to internalize cost externalities through taxes or fines and to internalize benefit externalities through public subsidies.

However, to *laissez-faire* advocates, the notion that extensive laws, taxes, and subsidies are necessary to maintain the efficiency of competitive markets in the face of external effects is quite troublesome. We know that Adam Smith, in *The Theory of Moral Sentiments*, argued that people have shared moral sentiments. In other words, they sympathize with each other to work many problems (externalities) out among themselves. Ronald Coase, a Nobel laureate affiliated with the University of Chicago later in his career, expanded upon this idea in the "The Problem of Social Cost" (1960).

According to the now famous Coase Theorem, *externalities will naturally tend to internalize themselves as long as transaction costs are low and property rights are tradable.* People continually interact and negotiate according to Coase. If a neighbor is creating a negative externality, as long as the parties involved can get together rather easily and talk, differences will be resolved through offers and exchanges. The same is true of positive externalities. His most famous example is beekeepers and orchard owners. Each need the other's resources, and each may seek compensatory payments from each other. Who pays whom depends upon property rights. However, regardless of who actually pays whom, the Coase Theorem emphasizes such private bargaining will give rise to efficient market solutions.

The Coase Theorem challenges the belief that extensive government rules to reduce spillover effects will create greater economic efficiency. Just the opposite is the case according to Coase. An individualistic, free-spirit, live-and-let-live philosophy is the answer according to University of Chicago economists.

Monopolies and Schumpeter's Forces of Creative Destruction

The fear that the unregulated markets can be rigged and controlled through monopoly power is found throughout modern economic thought. A famous passage in the *Wealth of Nations* states, "People of the same trade seldom meet together, even for merriment and diversion, but the conversation ends in a conspiracy against the public or in some contrivance to raise prices." Marx railed against the monopolistic exploitation of the working class. Even Marshall condemned monopoly power in a simple demand-supply setting.

Figure 3.5 shows Marshall's view of monopolizing a competitive industry in which demand and cost (supply) conditions remain the same before and after monopolization. The effect is to reduce output from Q_{PC} to Q_M and to raise prices from P_{PC} to P_M.

Figure 3.5: Standard Equilibrium Comparison Between Pure Competition and Pure Monopoly

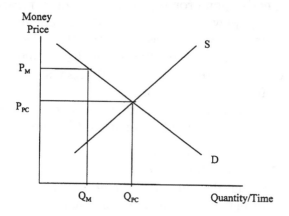

Economists at the turn of the century called for two government solutions to monopoly power in order to create a more level playing field. One was to make extensive use of antitrust policy. In the U.S., the Sherman Act appeared in 1890, quickly followed by the Clayton Act in 1914. These cornerstones of U.S. antitrust action make illegal either monopolization or attempts to monopolize and outlaw price fixing, interlocking directorates, tying contracts, detrimental forms of price discrimination, stock buy-outs of rivals, and the formation of domestic cartels.

The second solution called for the government to regulate the price and output of *natural monopolies*. A natural monopoly arises when having one large supplier appears to create major cost advantages over having many small producers. Water and electric companies are frequent examples since duplication of their facilities is expensive. Antitrust policy will create many small, inefficient producers, so the argument is for a *government-regulated monopoly*. A firm is granted a government franchise to be the sole monopoly supplier in a given area, and in return a regulatory body or commission specifies selling price, determines allowable expenses, and sets a "fair" rate of return for the firm.

In the 1930's, New Deal policies and Keynesian economics fanned the flames for greater use of antitrust and natural-monopoly regulation to offset the evils of extensive market power. *Laissez-faire* reasoning was under intense siege. Then into the fray steps one of the most forceful defenders of modern capitalism, Joseph Schumpeter. His arguments are found in *Business Cycles*, published in 1939, and subsequently in the more widely read *Capitalism, Socialism, and Democracy*, published in 1942.

Schumpeter was an individual of boundless energy, a cosmopolitan lifestyle and outlook, and an intense love of personal freedom. His *theory of creative destruction* reflects these ideas. Wild, crazy innovators first *create* monopoly profits, then the gale force winds of competition *destroy* them. Subsequently, another cycle begins.

Specifically, suppose a dynamic, capitalist economy is at *general equilibrium*. This means: (1) desired demand equals desired supply in all product, resource, and financial markets; and (2) all firms are making normal profits, as opposed to above-normal or monopolistic profits, so that they are just covering their opportunity costs of time and money of being in business. The first condition means prices and quantities are at rest in all markets, and the second condition means firms are at rest in all markets (none want to enter a particular market nor to leave). Thus the economy is at a *general state of rest*. Obviously, general equilibrium is a hypothetical situation, but it is Schumpeter's theoretical starting point.

Now suppose a major innovation comes along, for example the railroad in the U.S. in the first part of the 19th century. Entrepreneurs or risk-takers, whom Schumpeter calls "social deviants", begin to supply that product to consumers. In the process, some of the firms, the "best" ones, will make huge monopoly profit. So will key suppliers to innovative industry. The railroad industry generated monopoly profits for various railroad barons, and for steel and lumber barons as well. This expansionary phase is the *creative* part of the business cycle according to Schumpeter. And it may last for years.

However, the above-normal profits will attract new firms. As they enter the industry, the competitive forces so aptly described by Smith and Marshall begin to take hold. This will cause the inevitable weeding out of inefficient producers and the reduction of monopoly profits in the industry. This contractionary phase is the *destruction* part of the business cycle. Eventually, the economy returns to another general equilibrium of normal profits and equilibrium prices, and the process starts anew.

Along comes another major innovation, like the automobile in the U.S. at the turn of the century. The process of creative destruction marches onward, with the forces of entrepreneurship and innovation trying to stay ahead of the forces of competition and profit-destruction. At times monopoly forces rule, investment spreads from industry to industry, and powerful economic booms are the result. At other times, competitive forces rule, firms face contractionary times, and downturns occur in the economy.

Due to the perceived inevitability of business cycles in capitalistic economics, Schumpeter's theory of creation destruction has very strong ideas about monopolies and appropriate government intervention. According to the theory:

- Only two types of monopolies persist in the long run: government created monopolies, typically detrimental rather than helpful to consumers, and highly innovative private-sector monopolies, which are at the cutting edge of their market, play by the rules, and deserve their profits rather than having them expropriated by misguided government actions.
- The attempt by the government to smooth out business cycles through interventionist policies has two significant opportunity costs. First, there is slower economic growth in the long run. Second, it creates a loss of personal freedom!

- *Inventors* are the people who come up with the ideas. In contrast, *innovators* are the risk takers, the social deviants who must be tolerated and permitted to live lifestyles out of the norm. Overtaxing and over regulating these entrepreneurs harms economic growth.
- The fundamental threat to mature, free-market, democratic economies is inflation, created by the government, in order to appease losers in the business cycle while trying to smooth out its effects.

A fervent desire is that all members of the U.S. House and Senate plus all federal judges and antitrust prosecutors fully understand Schumpeter's theory of creative destruction. Indeed, they must to pass a test on creative destruction and free markets before deciding on any tax, monopoly, or regulatory issue. Well-intentioned attempts to punish successful social deviants/ entrepreneurs carry a devastating opportunity cost to society. The instigators of innovative change are driven underground, and personal freedom is lost.

Flows of Knowledge and Hayek's Insights

Marshallians analyzed pure and perfect competition. *Pure* competition means a "homogeneous" good sold by a "large" number of buyers and sellers. *Perfect* competition adds to pure competition the assumptions of perfect resource mobility (no barriers to entry) and perfect knowledge by firms and households about market demand and cost conditions.

Certainly, significant degrees of knowledge have to arise if the highest quality and widest array of items are to keep flowing into the marketplace at competitive prices. At the same time, we all know that perfect knowledge does not exist in the real world. The Great Depression, combined with the greater planning efforts of WWII, generated sentiment among economists that the federal government must step directly into markets, gather demand and supply information, and then set prices at something close to the competitive ideal. In other words, the government can speed up the flow of market knowledge through central planning.

In 1945, at the very height of the war efforts, F. A. Hayek wrote one of the most insightful economic articles ever to appear, "The Use of Knowledge in Society". The fundamental premise is that knowledge is itself a commodity in the market-place. It is produced and consumed, and useful knowledge has significant opportunity costs. Moreover, two basic types of knowledge flow throughout the economy, we'll call them *scientific* and *day-to-day*.

Scientific knowledge comes from research labs, think tanks, and universities. Such knowledge is verifiable and often quite precise regarding natural laws and principles. It has played a key role in transforming daily life of the masses of society. University faculty and other high-level professional practition-ers are enamored with scientific knowledge, wanting to spread its truths far and wide. The wondrous process of creative destruction cannot take place without scientific knowledge.

There is also the *day-to-day* knowledge, the *here-and-now* knowledge. Everyone faces unique alternatives, unique oppor-tunity costs, and unique constraints. This is what makes each of us special consumers/producers and creates comparative advan-tages. Day-to-day knowledge is often dismissed by formal sci-entists as relatively unimportant. Yet, as Hayek emphasized, it is day-to-day knowledge that underlines the voluntary exchange of goods and services: "Ultimate decisions must be left to the people who are familiar with these circumstances and who know directly of the relevant changes and of the resources immediately available to them."

What is so interesting about free markets, according to Hayek, is how the human race stumbled upon them serendipi-tously rather than through careful scientific method. Perhaps this is the reason many scientists seem disdainful of unfettered capitalism. The market process works so well, as Adam Smith recognized, because of the autonomous pursuit of individual happiness. As relative prices adjust in response to shifts in demand or supply, buyers and sellers respond in ways that only they know why at the moment.

For this reason, it is impossible for the government to gather the day-to-day knowledge necessary to set prices to clear all markets. No single mind, or for that matter no group of minds, *no matter how brilliant*, can set "better" prices than the seeming chaos of a free market. To believe otherwise is either extreme arrogance or extreme stupidity. Hayek's paradoxical conclusion is that as the government tries to speed up the flow of useful knowledge in society (for example through price manipulation or regulatory agencies like the Food and Drug Administration) it actually slows down useful knowledge. Like any scarce commodity, useful knowledge is produced and used most efficiently in a competitive rather than a government-regulated environment.

Given its tremendous insights, Hayek's article should be required reading by more than politicians or judges. It should be read by anyone interested in economic debates about the functioning of an economy. Its fundamental themes become ever more luminescent as the complexity of modern life intensifies.

Concluding Remarks

We now have a strong sense of the philosophy of free markets and neoclassical microeconomic principles. Marshall, Coase, Schumpeter, and Hayek are brilliant thinkers. But you may want to see the philosophy in action. Contrary to popular opinion, the majority of professional economists don't spend most of their time formulating highly mathematical, esoteric theories that exist only in hyperspace. Instead, basic principles are applied to everyday life and described in words! Four such applications are provided in the appendices for your possible entertainment and amusement: roads markets, office markets, ticket markets, and children markets. Chapter Five further extends the pricing and market discussions begun in this chapter.

APPENDIX 3A

THE U.S. ROAD AND DRIVING MARKET

From certain markets we can learn a great deal about ourselves, both individually and collectively. The U.S. driving market is a perfect example. It highlights the balance in the government setting rules and regulations in order to improve day-to-day life. It also tells volumes about individual personalities.

Just think of the relatively "free" nature of the U.S. road system. Most roads don't charge tolls (although some congested areas like Los Angeles now have toll roads where charges vary by time of day being used). To participate as a driver, you are suppose to have a valid license, but even this is not absolutely necessary. Indeed, about the only barrier to entry is not having a working vehicle with gas. The result is a growing market demand for a relatively fixed supply of roads. In addition, the demand for particular roads varies considerably by time of day, time of year, and other factors. Overall, U.S. roads are typically allocated on a first-come-first-served basis.

Externalities from other drivers are everywhere! Noise, air pollution, congestion, and road-rage abound. Traffic is never-ending stop-and-go. To protect life and limb, there are government laws about pollution, required safety equipment, the imposition of speed limits, and the use of road signs (to reduce bargaining costs). Still, this is a market based essentially on TRUST among the participants since even one mistake can be fatal. Adam Smith's shared moral sentiments constrain dangerous driving behavior in most of us.

Choice is abundant even with all the constraints present. Consumers can make decisions on the times of day to be on given roads. There are motorcycles, economy cars, midsize cars, luxury cars, trucks, and minivans, all of which are highly personalized. You can be a highly aggressive driver, or you can carefully obey all laws (and be screamed and gestured at). You can give other drivers an opening or you can cut them off. Broadly speaking, you can be either a BLOCKER or a MOVER on the roads.

Drivers may not have perfect knowledge about the roads about to be entered. Accidents, major construction delays, or natural hazards arise. But information may be acquired quickly, for example by listening to a radio traffic report. For the roads near where you live, you have built up important day-to-day knowledge over time about the most efficient and safest routes to take.

How the government gets involved beyond basic rules to minimize externalities is open to intense debate. Should there be uniform federal speed limits? What about imposing even stricter pollution, gas mileage, or safety standards for vehicles? Should the government raise taxes to build more roads that allow "free" access? Or should more tolls be used in congested areas according to the time of day? Should the use of car pooling lanes be encouraged even when the true-blooded American attitude appears to be "one person-one car"? And what about subsidizing mass public transportation? In a scarce world, these debates will never end, and freedom on the roads remains a relative concept.

APPENDIX 3B

ALLOCATION OF FACULTY OFFICES

All departments in a college are about to move into new office suites, where half the offices in any suite have windows and half do not. What is the "best" approach to allocating the offices among faculty members? Consider the following story of the Arizona State University College of Business, written with my colleague, Bill Boyes, which appeared in the *Journal of Economic Perspective* in 1989.

Auctions as an Allocation Mechanism in Academia: The Case of Faculty Offices

A six-story addition to Arizona State University's College of Business was completed in 1983, causing entire departments to be uprooted and relocated. Faculty offices had to be reassigned as a result. What seemed to be a trivial problem, the allocation of offices, turned out to be a very complex one. This is the story of how that problem was resolved.

In the new facility each suite of offices contains an equal number of internal and external offices. The internal offices are windowless while the external offices each have one wall of windows, making the differences between internal and external offices quite significant. In addition to the potential for claustrophobia in the internal offices, the topography of Phoenix turns anything above two stories into a terrific vantage point. And since many faculty view their offices in a manner similar to how middle management in private industry views the size of desks—a symbol that signals their importance to others in the organization the assignment of offices took on a flavor of a crucial decision.

Given the importance of the offices and the relative scarcity of choice locations, administrators faced a problem of allocation: How were the offices to be assigned? One of the most interesting aspects of observing management in an academic setting is the difficulty the system has with such decisions. Reliance on the market system in academia is virtually nonexistent. The incentives run counter to those of a private market; even in the case of the budgeting process it is common to find non-fungibility from year to year and often from line item to line item, thus ensuring a lack of incentives for spending anything less than the entire budget allocation before the end of the fiscal year. Not unexpectedly, then, the departments in the College of Business at ASU became a microcosm of the world of alternative allocative systems in their attempt to reassign offices.

The Management Department had no doubts about how to allocate its offices. Viewing itself as the decision-making leader of the College of Business, the department's chairman immediately ordained that offices would be assigned on the basis of "seniority"— defined as the length of time spent at ASU. The member of the Management Department with the longest ASU employment would have first choice, the second longest the second choice and so on until new incoming assistant professors received the remaining offices. The Marketing and Accounting Departments quickly followed the lead of the Management Department and adopted seniority as their allocation mechanism.

As might be expected, not all faculty members in these departments were satisfied with the outcomes. Some professors, who through luck or successful rent-seeking had obtained the best offices in the old facility, ended up with poorer offices in the new facility and complained vehemently. Assistant professors argued that given the demands to do research, they had to spend long hours in the office; therefore they deserved the better locations far more than older professors who rarely used their offices.

The chairman of the Finance Department noticed the squabbling that occurred in the Accounting, Marketing, and Management Departments and decided to forego the seniority mechanism. Instead, he posted a sign-up sheet outside his office one day without any warning. Faculty offices were chosen in order of signature on the sign-up sheet. In theory, nobody would be excluded *a priori* from getting one of the better offices. In reality, the system was biased toward those who walked past the chairman's bulletin board most often. Those professors sequestered in their offices carrying out research failed to see the sign-up sheet. Those faculty out of town, on sabbatical, on leave of absence, or ill ended up with the last choices. After the allocation, many argued that the system favored those "homeless" professors who simply wander the halls looking for distractions.

The chairman of the Statistics Department, realizing the deficiencies with the seniority mechanism and the problems with the "shock" technique of arbitrarily posting a sign-up sheet, decided to roll dice. This was initially met with excitement since everyone would start with an equal chance for the best offices. However, grumbling soon developed as those with the better offices in the old building began to fear a welfare loss through no fault of their own and with no way to offset the loss. The actual outcome of the dice experiment confirmed the fears. A recall of the initial allocation occurred and the use of the seniority system resulted.

The Economics Department was also affected by the reassignment. (In fact, the systems were put in place nearly simultaneously rather than the sequential order we're discussing in this paper). The chairman, Boyes, wanted to minimize rent-seeking by individual faculty members and recognized that rationing by price would achieve this as well as lead to efficiencies not associated with other allocative mechanisms. Consequently, he decided to create a market environment for the sale of offices. But without private property rights to the offices, and faced with the political constraints of an academic institution, it was necessary to step carefully into a situation where a market system could be used.

A request for suggestions on how to allocate the offices was sent to the department faculty. Perhaps not surprisingly, given that academics (even economists) are not used to thinking of allocations within their institutions in terms of a market system, none of the suggestions included rationing by price. The "serious" schemes proposed included one from the senior member of the department who said that there was only one way to allocate the offices, the way it had been done at great institutions for centuries, on the basis of seniority. Other proposals, some made with tongue in cheek, were to base the allocation on research productivity, teaching effectiveness, height, weight, race, sex, and religion. One member even suggested a brawl—called office wrestlemania. With no suggestions related to the creation of a market and with no information regarding the value of an office, the chairman decided to rely on an auction as the allocation mechanism.

The question then became the kind of auction to undertake. The literature suggested a number of possibilities, including oral auctions (English or Dutch) and sealed-bid auctions (single or repeated bids). Since the main concern of the chairman was to minimize transaction costs and rent-seeking rather than to maximize revenue, a single sealed-bid auction was chosen as the allocation mechanism.[1]

Faculty were informed that three weeks hence, every faculty member in the department could submit a single sealed bid. The highest bid would receive the first choice, and so on down the line. Those who chose not to submit a bid would be guaranteed an office, but they would choose last. Ties would be broken by random selection. After an office was "purchased," the faculty member owned the property rights to that office as long as he or she remained at ASU. If the faculty member was away from campus for leave or sabbatical, the office could be rented but would not be confiscated (previously offices could be and often were reassigned). In addition, offices could be subleased to other faculty or visitors as opportunities arose.

The proceeds from the auction were used to create a fund for graduate student scholarships, travel, and dissertation support. Although most faculty members saw this as worthwhile, there was very little expressed interest in where the money actually went as long as the chairman didn't pocket it. Half of the proceeds from subsequent rents or subleases would also go to the scholarship fund, but the remaining 50 percent would be returned to the faculty member in the faculty member's budget allocation.[2]

The three-week interval gave members of the department the opportunity to seek information regarding the elasticity of demand for window offices and to attempt to form cartels. Once the 24 bids were submitted and opened, the allocation went smoothly. The highest bid was $500, the next highest bid was

$250, the cut-off for a window office was $75, and a total of $3200 was raised. The only ex post complaint came from the highest bidder who, in a winner's curse, paid twice what the second place bidder paid.

The experiment was a raging success until one of the authors, Happel, decided to relay the allocation process and its subtleties to his principles courses. The auction provided valuable lessons regarding the incentives for not allowing a market environment to arise in academic settings as well as the standard lessons on the efficiency of the market process. Students readily grasped the idea that the price mechanism undermines the power of university administrators and realized that how the money was actually spent is irrelevant in terms of achieving an efficient allocation scheme. One of the students, who happened to be a reporter from the ASU campus newspaper, published the story on the front page of the newspaper. The story was picked up by the Phoenix media and then by media elsewhere. While the department seemed to enjoy the outcome and notoriety that accompanied the experiment, the chairman had to face the onslaught of the central administration and the local public. This was exactly the type of publicity that an administration reeling from a series of problems with the athletic program wanted to avoid. They were not able to deflect the allegation that public property had been sold. During the ensuing weeks, a great deal of energy was devoted to pointing out the costs and benefits of the market mechanism and other allocation mechanisms to these administrators and to the general public. Yet, it was due only to the fact that the money collected had gone into a scholarship fund that the controversy eventually dissipated without serious recriminations.

Since the initial reallocation in 1983, the negative
aspects of the experiment have virtually disappeared
and even the central administration now appears to
think it novel and interesting. Since the first auction,
three window offices have been vacated. Sealed bids
for these offices have yielded much higher prices than
did the initial auction, with the average final sale price
of $350. For those faculty members with a strong
desire for a window office, the acquisition of such an
office in 1983 appears to be one of the better spending
decisions that they made the past five years as the
average price increase has been about 25 percent per
year. And while the purchase price is rising steadily,
those of you passing through Arizona for a short stay
may wish to inquire about rental rates. They are quite
reasonable, especially during the low-tourism season.

[1] *Given that there were no untenured faculty in the department at the
time and that only two members were within six years of retirement,
the expected lives at ASU of all participants was about the same. The
auction, therefore, was not biased against specific groups of faculty.*

[2] *The same year of the auction an annual budget allocation was begun.
Each faculty member was assigned a fund from which travel, copy-
ing, journal subscriptions, and so on could be financed. Any funds
remaining at year end could (at some rate less than one) be carried
over to the next year.*

APPENDIX 3C

TICKET SCALPING

Ticket scalping is typically defined as charging a higher price than the face value printed on the ticket. It is condemned in public, especially by politicians, as unfair to the "average" fan. Why should consumers have to pay more than the "legal" price? Do you agree with this reasoning? Before you say yes or no, consider the following article written with my colleague, Marianne Jennings, that appeared in the *Wall Street Journal* (February 23, 1995).

Herd Them Together and Scalp Them

By Stephen K. Happel And Marianne M. Jennings

PHOENIX—Troubled by the outrageous prices scalpers were getting for his concert tickets, Garth Brooks developed a lottery system for his concert here. If you stood in line long enough, you had a shot at the $25 tickets. When the lottery was completed, the singer was stunned to see scalpers getting $500 for the same seats in the secondary market. "I've seen the show," he said. "It's not worth it."

But from Broadway to the Super Bowl, it is worth it. Scalpers thrive because of the demand for live, limited-seating events. They tap a market of buyers whose time is in short supply but whose money isn't.

Despite the economic role of scalpers, they have been consistently treated as pariahs over the past century in the U.S. Currently 26 states, the District of Columbia, and most municipalities with professional sports franchises regulate scalping in some way.

Some laws set maximum ticket resale prices. Others outlaw scalping at or near the event site or require a costly license to do so. Still others limit legal scalping to charitable organizations. Such market restrictions are supposed to legislate "fair" prices so that the "average" fan can attend, or at least eliminate the congestion on the streets leading to arenas. But harnessing free enterprise is a tall order. Sooner or later something has to give. And during the past two weeks it did in a big way in Phoenix.

In response to the high levels of ticket scalping and traffic congestion outside the America West Arena, home of the Suns basketball team, the City Council passed an ordinance early this month that allows scalping, no license required, to take place in a designated area across the street from the main entrance to the arena; everywhere else scalping is still illegal. Thus Phoenix became the first municipality in the U.S. to openly encourage scalping at the event site and to centralize the market.

The innovative ordinance was not passed without opposition. The position of the Phoenix Suns and their president and CEO, Jerry Colangelo, was that any form of ticket scalping not licensed by the National Basketball Association and the Suns should not be permitted. The Suns management, along with downtown merchants, wanted police to use existing laws that prohibit street vending without a license. Management last year had been able to establish through a federal court decision that a Suns season ticket holder has purchased only a license from the Suns, and this license can be revoked if the tickets are sold above their face value.

The police, who previously favored legalizing scalping, since enforcement was so difficult, worried that scuffles would be more commonplace in a centralized market. But citizens at the public hearing argued that people might actually be safer in one spot under the watchful eye of the police, and that a free market was the best way to ensure that the average person could get good seats. The public outcry resulted in an 8-1 vote for the ordinance.

The NBA All-Star Game on Feb. 12 gave the new Phoenix scalpers' market its first run. On game day, the police swept through the downtown area in the morning and issued warnings to scalpers not selling in the designated area. With the scalpers gathered into a one-stop shopping- forum buyers could easily gather information from all sellers. Some sellers simply stood passively with one or two tickets in hand. Others held signs advertising seat locations and prices. The professional traders, with large numbers of tickets, aggressively shouted out prices and moved through the crowd seeking customers. In total, some 400 scalpers traded in the designated area in the five-hour period before the game; half of them were professionals. and of the professionals at least 150 were from out of town.

Present were all the trappings of a buyers' market. Prices for $100 face-value upper-deck seats that sold earlier in the week for $450 were fetching $300 two hours before the game and $150 at tip-off. Seventh-row seats that sold on Saturday for $1,000 went for $500 two hours before tip-off. One professional scalper complained in the newspapers, "We can't make nothing." In other words, the new open market produced remarkable yet predictable results. With supply and demand in one place, buyers shopped and sellers hustled-scuffle-free. It was reminiscent of the humble Wall Street beginnings of the stock exchange.

Jerry Colangelo came out on the arena's balcony to look upon the secondary market in operation. Appropriately, he was joined by Rush Limbaugh, perhaps the most outspoken advocate of capitalism in America today. They watched market reallocation.

Appendix 3C

They studied demand and supply. They witnessed free
enterprise and a market-based solution to scalping.
something that had evaded a century of legislation: If
you can't beat the scalpers. put them all in one place
and let them compete. The two men smiled.

APPENDIX 3D

THE CHICAGO-COLUMBIA APPROACH TO FERTILITY AND BECKER'S ROTTEN KID THEOREM

One of the truly clever minds in microeconomic theory belongs to Nobel laureate Gary Becker. In "An Economic Analysis of Fertility" (1960), he ventured into the household fertility decision-making process in developed countries, and, as a result the Chicago-Columbia approach was born.

According to Becker, rational households "choose" family size in developed countries. Due to child-labor laws, mandatory schooling, and government old-age security pensions, couples are not having children to work in the fields or care for the elderly. Instead, they are having children essentially for consumption purposes. They may be "gifts of God" or "the most cherished visitors in your home", but fundamentally children are consumer durable goods, so they are subject to the basic laws of microeconomics.

Becker assumes that children have no close consumption substitutes and are truly *normal goods* rather than *inferior goods*. Holding everything else constant, rising household incomes, therefore, imply larger family sizes. Yet, across countries, richer nations have smaller average family sizes than less wealthy nations, and within developed countries like the U.S. richer households typically have fewer children than poorer households. Children appear to be inferior goods.

Becker's answer to this paradox is straightforward neo-classical reasoning. The "full price" of a child is comprised of its money price and its time price. As household income goes up, if everything else remains the same, couples will demand more children because they are normal. However, everything else doesn't remain the same. First, the higher household income raises the opportunity cost of parents' time, which means time-intensive goods like children become quite pricey. Second, the increase in household income causes the money price of children to rise as well. The higher income leads parents to demand more "child-quality" expenditures, such as private schools and music lessons that enhance a child's abilities, talents, or self-confidence. When combined, the time effect and the quality effect from the increase in household income raises the full price of children such that the normal good effect is being swamped. Well-to-do households end up "choosing" fewer children. Fertility rates are low, near replacement levels, in developed countries simply because of the Law of Demand. The fundamentals of Marshallian price theory prevail.

A thought-provoking idea coming out of this methodology is the *rotten kid theorem*. Becker assumes that all households have a "head", either a male or female (or both), who wish to keep the household intact and who worry deeply about everyone else's utility. Being rational, the head allocates the scarce resources of the household—money and time— so that each member of the household is equally well-off at the margin. For instance, the last dollar spent for the head's consumption must yield the same marginal utility as the last dollar spent on either the spouse or other children. Otherwise, resources should be reallocated until equimarginalism prevails.

Suppose now that there is an extremely greedy or rotten kid who wants everything in sight. The child may discover, however, that constantly asking for goodies leads to a parental rebuff from the head: "No, you can't have everything you want. Look at your brothers and sisters – they need things too. Why don't you share more?" Consequently, the extremely greedy child quickly learns that "acting" altruistically leads to better results than demonstrating rotten behavior. Greedy behavior is disguised.

What an argument! The invisible hand is operating intensely at the level of the family. With the proper inducements or household constraints, extremely greedy and selfish behavior can be turned into altruism and benevolence!

The Chicago-Columbia approach has since added rational models of marriage, divorce, the timing and spacing of births, and generational endowments to the new home economics. It is a testament to the human mind to carry a particular train of thought to the very depths and crevices of day-to-day life using mathematics in ways to draw contemporary conclusions.

[Painting] is easy when you
don't know how, but very
difficult when you do.
Edgar Degas

CHAPTER FOUR

PRICING DECISIONS BY FIRMS

Economists are fascinated by prices—how they are set, the signals they send, and the optimality or disutility they can create. How often do we as consumers see a price of an item and wonder why that particular price? At times we have some idea of what is going on, but at other times it is confusing. This chapter lays out modern economic theory of pricing decisions by firms.

The discussion begins with the foundations: demand elasticities in relation to marginal revenue and marginal costs in relation to average costs and total profits. Next, long-run equilibrium models are depicted for typical firms in pure competition, monopolistic competition, oligopoly, nondiscriminating pure monopoly, and discriminating pure monopoly. Throughout static equilibria are contrasted with dynamic considerations.

The discussion then turns to the more intuitive side of microeconomics. How can the models be used as a guide to real-world pricing decisions? Analyzed here are incremental versus full-cost pricing, pricing a new product, multiproduct pricing for final goods, and transfer pricing for intermediate goods. At all times a marginalist perspective dominates.

Foundations

To determine pricing outcomes in the modern marketplace, where better to begin than with demand elasticities.

Demand Elasticities and Marginal Revenue

Let's return to the basic market demand curve first encountered in Figure 3.1. It is reproduced in figure 4.1.

Figure 4.1: Market Demand Curve and
Its Elasticities for a Final Good or Service

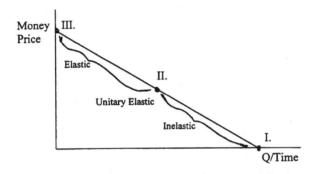

This market demand curve, a negatively-sloped straight line that touches both axes, is the summation of all individual demand curves for the product in the time period in question. Extensive microeconomic theory in the form of indifference curves, household budget constraints, and utility maximization is used to derive individual demand curves. "Consumer sovereignty" is assumed.

Out of this microeconomic bag of tricks comes *price elasticity*. Elasticity, in general, is the percentage change in one variable caused by a percentage change in another variable, *ceteris paribus*. Because it is a percentage rather than absolute change, units of measurement cancel out and a "pure" number emerges. Oranges can literally be compared to apples.

Price elasticity (PE) is the percentage change in desired quantity purchased caused by a percentage change in price, *ceteris paribus*:

Chapter 4

$$-\left[\frac{\frac{\Delta Q}{Q}}{\frac{\Delta P}{P}}\right]=-\left[\frac{\Delta Q}{\Delta P}\right]\left[\frac{P}{Q}\right].$$

Because price and desired quantity move inversely due to the Law of Demand, the minus sign converts PE into a positive value. The numerical value of PE is equal to the slope of the demand curve (a constant for a straight line) times a particular P over its associated Q.

The purpose of PE is to convey consumer intensity. If 0≤PE<1, demand is "inelastic." A relative change in price, say 10%, causes less than a 10% change in quantity. Indeed, it might cause no change in quantity, so PE=0 and demand is "perfectly inelastic." If PE=1, demand is "unitary elastic." A percentage change in price causes an exact offsetting change in quantity desired. Finally, if PE>1, demand is "elastic." A given change in price, say 10%, causes a larger percentage change in quantity than 10%. Demand responds and stretches to relative price changes. Indeed, as PE→∞ (approaches infinity), demand becomes "perfectly elastic."

In Figure 4.1, all three ranges of price elasticity exist on the demand curve. At point I demand is perfectly inelastic ($\frac{\Delta Q}{\Delta P}$, the slope, is constant, Q is a positive value, and P is zero). Up to point II demand remains inelastic. At point II demand turns to unitary elastic. In the upper half of the demand curve is elastic, and it is perfectly elastic at point III.

There are three critical themes here. The first is that price elasticity will change over price ranges with a "typical" demand curve. Demand is inelastic at relatively low prices and elastic at higher prices.

Carrying this a step further, the second theme is that the shape of the demand curve affects price elasticity. Figure 4.2 depicts a demand curve that has unitary elasticity throughout. IT IS TRULY A CURVE (specifically, a rectangular hyperbola that approaches but never touches both axis). As relative price falls from P* to P**, the percentage change in quantity from Q* to

Q** is exactly the same. In contrast, Figure 4.3 depicts a perfectly inelastic demand curve in which consumers buy Q* no matter the price is in the relevant range, wheras Figure 4.4 depicts a perfectly elastic demand curve where even a slight increase in price causes the firm to lose all sales. Figure 4.5 depicts elastic demand at the relevant price P* where a slight decrease in price leads to a substantial increase in sales and a slight increase in price causes customers to jump to other sellers. There can even be a "kinked" demand curve at the current price P*, as in Figure 4.6, where the firm fears that a price increase causes a very elastic response as customers run to rivals and that a price decrease causes a very inelastic response as rivals match price cuts.

Figure 4.2: Unitary Elastic Demand Curve

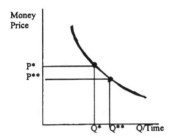

Figure 4.3: Perfectly Inelastic Demand Curve

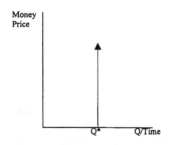

Figure 4.4: Perfectly Elastic Demand Curve

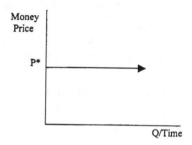

Figure 4.5: Firm Facing Elastic Demand

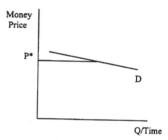

Figure 4.6: A Kinked Demand Curve

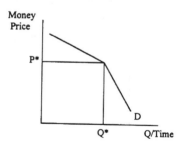

Besides the price range itself, what other factors directly affect the elasticity of final goods and services? The number of viable substitutes is often considered the most important factor, with more substitutes meaning more elastic demand. The percent of the budget that is devoted to the good or service also has a big impact at times, with the larger percent leading to more elastic demand and price sensitivity. And, the longer the time period involved, the more elastic is demand because of the greater opportunity to shop around.

The third critical theme here is that, with the typical straight-line downward sloping demand in Figure 4.1, a profit-maximizing firm will want move to price out of the inelastic region into the elastic region of the demand curve. To understand why, we need to tie in the idea of marginal revenue. Figure 4.7 reproduces 4.1 with the marginal revenue (MR) curve where no price discrimination occurs.

Figure 4.7: The Market Demand Curve and the Marginal Revenue Curve for a Nondiscriminating Monopoly

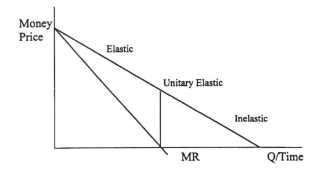

Recall that MR is the change in total revenue when one more unit of Q is sold. When demand is inelastic, MR is negative. Each additional unit sold causes total revenue to fall because the percentage decline in price is greater than the percentage increase in quantity. At the same time, each additional unit causes total costs to rise. Therefore, total profits must decrease if prices are cut with inelastic demand. So the firm keeps raising prices instead until all inelastic demand is eliminated and MR becomes zero.

At unitary elasticity, MR is zero. A price increase or decrease has no impact on total revenue. But additional price

increases mean total costs continue to decline as less is produced. Therefore, the profit maximizing level of output lies
somewhere in the elastic region of the demand curve. Exactly
where requires going to the per-unit level to find the point where
MR=MC. Only in the elastic region is MR positive.

Marginal Costs, Average Costs, and Profits or Loses

In Chapter Three the relationship between marginal costs
(MC), average variable costs (AVC) and average costs (AC) were
developed for a plant (a department store) that is subject at first
to division/specialization effects and then to the Law of
Diminishing Physical Returns. Figure 4.8 reproduces Figure 3.2
and introduces prices into the picture to show economic profits or losses.

Figure 4.8: Profits or Losses in the Short Run

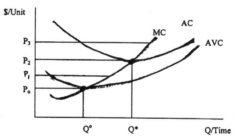

We start by recognizing that only at Q* does MC equal AC:
at levels of output to the left MC<AC, and at levels to the right
MC>AC. A profit-maximizing firm will not produce in the short
run if it does not cover AVC, which means it does not produce at
prices below P_0. At P_0, the firm is just covering its AVC, which is
enough to keep it in business in the short run. The firm's supply
curve begins at this point.

At prices between P_0 and P_1, a firm suffers losses even if
P=MC because P<AC. The firm remains in business, however,
because P>AVC and a contribution is being made to overhead.

At P_2, here and here alone price is equal to both AC and MC. Assuming that AC include all opportunity costs, then P=AC means equity: no economic profits or losses, just *normal profits* that cover the opportunity costs of remaining in business. Lastly, for all prices above P_1, for example P_2, P>AC even if P=MC and a firm enjoys economic profits.

To repeat one final time, price equals MC doesn't tell you a thing about whether the firm is making economic profits or suffering losses. Price in relation to AC gives you that answer.

Yet price equals MC is often seen as the "best" price by free-market economists in terms of consumer welfare. Assuming that all externalities have been internalized, then MC represents the cost to society of producing one more unit of output and price represents the marginal benefit to society of consuming one more unit. As long as P>MC, then society wants more of the good. Only at P=MC is *social efficiency* achieved, in which added costs equal added benefits for the last unit consumed. Also, please keep in mind that P=MC doesn't guarantee that production takes place at the lowest point on the AC curve, Q*, the point of *productive efficiency*. Thus, P=MC, while desirable in sense, is not necessarily economic utopia.

Standard Microeconomic Pricing Models of The Four Basic Market Structures

Modern microeconomics distinguishes four types of market structures: pure (perfect) competition, monopolistic competition, oligopoly, and pure monopoly under both nonprice and price discrimination. In the following analysis, they are defined and then long-run equilibrium is depicted for each. Throughout this presentation:

- The cost curves are drawn the same way in all models. The differences in the models lie in the shape and position of the demand/marginal revenues, as determined by number of substitutes, barriers to entry, and rivals' reactions.
- In all models, equilibrium in where the MR curve intersects the MC curve. Always find this point!

- For *any* single firm in *any* of the four market structures, *anything* can happen in the short run: losses and close down, losses and stay in business, normal profits, or economic profits. It is the long run that is our focus.

Pure Competition

Pure competition is comprised of many buyers and sellers (numerous "price-takers") who view all firms' products as homogeneous. It turns into *perfect competition* if resources are completely mobile (no barriers to entry) and perfect knowledge flows. The typical competitive firm in relation to the market is shown in Figure 4.9.

Figure 4.9: Pure Competition in the Long Run

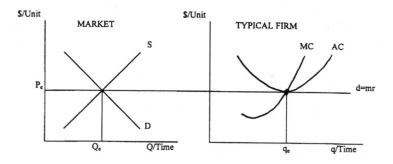

Because products are not differentiated in quality or service, even a 1 percent price increase causes the typical firm to lose all its sales. Thus, at the market equilibrium price P_e, the competitive firm's demand curve (d) is perfectly elastic. Since the firm can sell at it wants at the going market price, the constant price means p=mr for the typical firm.

The firm produces at mr=MC, and this occurs at q_e output. The sum of all these individual q_e's equals total market output of Q_e. In the long run, no barriers to entry and perfect knowledge cause economic profits to be eliminated. In addition, the most efficient plant is built under existing technology, and it is operated at its most efficient point, so there is complete productive efficiency. Finally, P=MC meaning social efficiency prevails as well.

Is it any wonder modern economists regard purely competitive markets so highly? Shifts in market conditions set off price adjustments in the short run that best deal with scarcity, and we come back to this beautiful equilibrium in the long run. The epitome of pure competition is futures and options trading, in which risk is spread around as goods and services "freely" exchange hands.

Monopolistic Competition

The model of *monopolistic competition* was developed by E.H. Chamberlin (1933), with Joan Robinson's (1933) "imperfect competition" conveying similar ideas. As in pure competition, monopolistically competitive markets have large numbers of buyers and sellers who think their actions go unnoticed with regard to price. Also, barriers to entry are minimal. However, firms have some brand loyalty—some monopoly power— because of *slight* product differentiation. Examples of monopolistic competition include supermarkets, drugstores, restaurants, bars, or gas stations in large urban areas, as well as various performing arts or entertainment industries. In his thorough analysis, Chamberlin first modeled pricing outcomes, then he turned to quality decisions and finally to advertising expenditures. Our focus is solely on his price theory.

Figure 4.10 presents Chamberlin's view of the demand conditions facing a typical firm. The overall market demand for the industry is divided among existing sellers. Because of the slight product differentiation, and because a typical believes that its pricing actions go unnoticed by rivals, at the existing price P_e it feels that demand is very elastic: a price cut will lead to a big increase in sales as it sells more to existing customers *and* it picks up some of other firms' customers because the products are close substitutes. The *expected* demand curve, as Chamberlin called it, is 11[1] in Figure 4.10.

Figure 4.10: Demand Curves for a
Monopolistic Competitive Firm

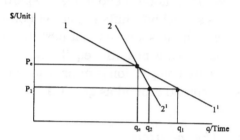

But if the typical firm expects that a price cut from P_e to P_1 will increase sales from q_e to q_1, all firms do. So they all cut price simultaneously to P_1 expecting to sell q_1 but selling q_2 (just more to existing customers). So the *actual* demand curve is 22'.

Figure 4.11 shows Chamberlin's market adjustment to long-run equilibrium. Suppose we start off with the expected-actual demand curves (11' and 22') at the top.

Figure 4.11: Monopolistic Competition
in the Long Run for the Typical Firm

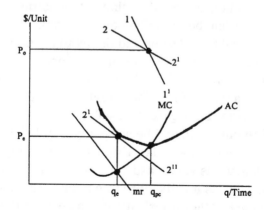

A price P_o with average costs AC imply large economic profits are being realized. Even so, existing firms cut price time and again in hopes of greater profits. Price wars become commonplace due to expectations. At the same time, new firms enter because barriers to entry are few.

Long-run equilibrium for the typical firm is P_e and q_e, with $2^1 2^{11}$ just tangent to the AC curve. (The actual demand curve at the point of tangency is left out). The price wars and easy entry have driven down P=AC. There are only normal profits and equity prevails.

However, there is also excess capacity. The reason is because of the product differentiation. Homogeneous products of pure competition lead to output q_{pc}. This loss of productive efficiency, according to Chamberlin, represents the opportunity costs to society of having greater choice. For example, the U.S. could have one national brand of gasoline like Mexico, thus eliminating 3 or 4 gas stations on busy corners, but we Americans love choice. Nothing is ever free. Chamberlin's idea known as the *Excess Capacity Theorem*, and it is a powerful insight to use on both friends and foes when defending free choice.

Oligopoly

"Oli" is the Greek word for few. In *oligopoly*, a few means more than one (a pure monopoly), but not so many that firms think their actions go unnoticed. The distinguishing feature of oligopoly is firms' *recognized interdependence* in the market in terms of pricing, advertising, market shares, barriers to entry, and quality.

Simple duopoly models can be traced back to Augustine Cournot, Joseph Bertrand, and F.Y. Edgeworth in the 19th century. But oligopoly is really a 20th century concept. Today probably the most recognized model is the Prisonners' Dilemma, first encountered in Chapter Two. Just as two prisoners weigh choices about confessing or not, so do firms about industry-versus-firm profits. Does one of them start price wars and other predatory practices that eventually hurts all significantly? Or do agreements come to stabilize the industry?

Chapter 4

The Prisonners' Dilemma is derived from *game theory*, developed by John von Neumann and Oskar Morgenstern (1944) starting in the late 1920's. A game consists of two or more players, sometimes in conflict and sometimes in cooperation, who are pursuing individual objectives in this group context. Some games are "zero-sum" like poker where total winnings equal total losses at the end of the evening. Other games are "non-zero sum," such as economic growth where a rising tide can lift all [non-leakable] ships. The sophistication and complexity of a game changes enormously depending upon the degree of cooperation present and the amount of useful information flowing freely rather than known only by individual players. Game theory's impact on understanding oligopolistic behavior has grown markedly over the past decade. Nobel Prizes have been recently awarded in this theoretical area to John Harsanyi, John Nash, Reinhard Selten (in 1994) and James Mirrlees and William Vickrey (in 1996).

Another widely recognized oligopolistic model is a *cartel*. Here a group of firms acts like a pure monopoly. Price is moved into the elastic region of the demand curve, and output is limited through quotas. While price fixing and domestic cartels are illegal according to U.S. antitrust laws, free-market economists believe cartels will break down rather quickly on their own due to the Prisonners' Dilemma. The strict production quotas necessary to maintain output restrictions eventually cause someone to cheat as excess capacity leads to price cuts. Let the marketplace sort things out.

At one time, perhaps the most famous model of oligopoly was Paul Sweezy's (1939) kinked demand curve, first seen in Figure 4.6 and redrawn in Figure 4.12. After a price P_e gets established, firms may come to fear that nobody will follow price increases and that everybody will match price decreases. Therefore, price stability can arise even if marginal costs conditions change considerably. The MR for the firm will be vertical over range directly under the kink; thus shifts from MC_1 to MC_2 to MC_3 have no impact on equilibrium price and output levels.

*Figure 4.12: The Kinked Demand
Curve Model of Price Stability*

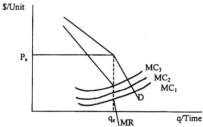

The recognition of kinked demand curve situations and volatile price expectations may cause oligopolistic firms to turn to price leadership. *Dominant price leadership* occurs when the biggest and most powerful firm, Walmart, sets prices and the smaller firms in the competitive fringe have to follow suit. In contrast, *barometric price leadership* (as in the airline industry) is where one firm tries our a price increase, and other firms may or may not follow the barometer.

I could go on with more oligopoly models that explore even deeper into individual complexities of markets, but you now understand the basic point. Surviving in oligopolistic markets requires constant vigilance of competitors. "Bad" decisions can set off price wars, drive customers to rivals, attract new firms, and, perish the thought, bring on the attention of antitrust regulators.

Nondisciminating Pure Monopoly

A *pure monopoly* means a single seller of a homogeneous product operating behind effective barriers to entry for an extended period of time. Pure monopolies are relatively rare. DeBeers' control of the diamond market is one example, and Microsoft with its Windows software is another.

The *nondiscriminating* pure monopoly model is shown in Figure 4.13. If the monopolist sells 1 unit of Q, price is $10.00. Two units sell for $18.00, meaning that the MR of the second unit is $8.00 even though its price is $9.00. Three units sell for $24.00, making marginal revenue of the third unit $6.00 even though its price is $8.00. The end result is that P>MR for the nondiscriminating monopolist.

Figure 4.13: Long Run Equilibrium for a Nondiscriminating Monopolist

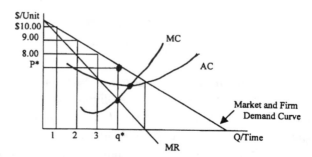

At the long-run equilibrium price P* and the output Q*, the monopolist is making economic profits. It is also operating with excess capacity. And with P>MR and MR=MC, P>MC it does not achieve social efficiency. Moreover, the profits and inefficiencies can continue as long as barriers to entry remain effective. Little wonder pure monopoly is so despised.

Yet you must keep in mind Schumpeter's theory of creative destruction before you are too ready to condemn monopolies. In a dynamic sense, if the large profits are heavily reinvested in product research and development that drives down average costs significantly, the price of the product can continue to fall for the consumer even though economic profits persist for extended periods of time. As Schumpeter stressed, only two types of monopolies last in the long run: government-created situations and *highly-innovative firms*.

Price Discriminating Monopolies by Degrees

Price discrimination, charging two or more different prices for essentially the same product for reasons other than cost differences, can only occur when a firm has some monopoly power. Purely competitive firms cannot price discriminate. For price discrimination to be successful, a firm must take advantage of different intensities (elasticities) of demand among consumers *and* must be able to seal or segment markets to prevent arbitrage. We will follow the ideas of C.A. Pigou (1920) and describe three forms of price discrimination.

First degree price discrimination is also known as the *perfectly discriminating monopolist*. It represents the most precise form of pricing—a different price is charged for each unit sold. This is accomplished through all-or-nothing offers based on the seller's reading of the buyers demand curve. Street vendors in border cities, ticket scalpers, and used car salesmen are examples. Figure 4.14 depicts the micro model of first degree price discrimination.

Figure 4.14: A Perfectly Discriminating Monoplolist

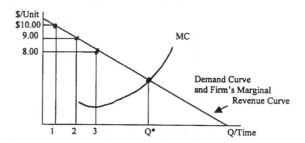

The first-degree price discriminator knows the demand curve perfectly. So instead of charging $10 for 1 unit, $9 for 2 units, and $8 for 3 units, the firm makes all-or-nothing offers. For one, it is $10; 2 are $19; and 3 are $27. Because the firm sells each additional unit without having to lower the prices on previous units, P=MR. The demand curve and marginal revenue curves are the same.

Accordingly, the firm produces Q*, more than the nondiscriminating pure monopolist. Indeed, social efficiency is achieved since P=MC for the last unit sold. The trade-off for achieving this efficiency is greater economic profits. Perfect price discriminators are often despised. But give them their due. They give rise to more output in the marketplace as they "fine-tune" prices.

Second degree price discrimination is also known as *block pricing*. Output is sold in blocks, for instance so much for the first number of kilowatt hours, a lower price for the next block, and so on. Second degree price discrimination is just a less extreme form of first degree. The MR curve moves closer to the market demand curve compared to a nondiscriminating pure monopolist, but it still lies below the demand curve. So once again, price discrimination leads to more output and greater efficiency than a nondiscriminating pure monopoly.

Third degree is the most common form of price discrimination in the real world. Here the seller recognizes two (or more) district demand curves for the product at a given moment, for instance kids and adults for movies. The market is segmented and the firm has two sets of demand and marginal revenue curves to deal with (two situations like Figure 4.7). How does the firm then proceed?

Let's use a movie theater charging adult and children prices as an example. The manager starts by assigning the first seat to the market with the highest marginal revenue, likely to be adults. The second seat is then allocated mentally. Again it might go to an adult. But sooner or later a seat is assigned to the child market due to it generating higher marginal revenue than the next adult seat sold. What the firm is doing is developing a *combined market revenue curve* (CMR) by going back and forth between the submarkets getting the highest possible marginal revenue for each additional unit of output. Setting this CMR equal to MC to maximize total profits, the firm allocates output in equilibrium such that the last purchaser is each submarket generates the same net MR for the firm. Otherwise, more seats should be allocated to the group generating the higher marginal. As you would expect, the submarket with the most elastic demand ends up paying the lowest price between the groups.

Extensions

To conclude our discussions of pricing, let's extend the basic models up to this to think intuitively about a number of issues in the real, day-to-day world of business. We'll begin with the most basic question of all. Are you going to be an incremental pricer? Then we'll consider new products and multiproduct firms. Finally, we'll address transfer pricing.

Incremental Versus Full Cost Pricing

Let's set the alternatives up as a black-and-white extremes. An *incremental pricer* knows the incremental (marginal) costs of producing another batch of output and is prepared to set prices equal to the incremental costs under certain conditions (excess capacity, declining market demand). At the same time, an incremental pricer is prepared to charge "what the market will bear" according to demand conditions. An incremental pricer is constantly seeking to "buy low and sell high" and abhors "leaving money on the table." An incrementalist and price discriminates whenever possible; indeed first degree price discrimination is the epitome.

In contrast, a *full cost pricer* (or *mark-up pricer* or *cost-plus pricer)* takes the average direct costs of production (or acquisition) and simply adds on a *pre-determined* markup. When asked why, full cost pricers argue that it is "fair" to all their customers—prices only go up when costs go up. Also, it is easier to use since firms often know more about actual cost information than exact demand conditions. And it guarantees a profit on each batch of output sold.

Naturally, free-market economists favor incremental pricing over full cost pricing. It enhances market efficiency and shows a flexibility on the part of firms, in contrast to the rigidity of full cost pricing. In the end, it's a question of attitude and outlook. Are you a true maximizer, and are you prepared to let market demand determine what is equitable?

Chapter 4

Pricing a New Product: Skimming Versus Penetration

Standard microeconomic theory normally does not draw a distinction between old and new products. But suppose that you are about to introduce a new product. You confront two basic choices as a profit maximizer: either to adopt a skimming approach or to adopt a penetration approach.

Skimming is starting with a high price, then lowering it over time. It's similar to first degree price discrimination in that the cream of the market is being skimmed. Those with the most intense demand pay the highest initial price, after which price is gradually lowered. In contrast, *penetration pricing* starts with an extremely low price to capture large shares of rivals customers immediately. Then the hope is to raise price as brand loyalty develops.

Economically, skimming is used when initial demand is considered very inelastic, but it is expected to become much more elastic over time. Graphite fishing rods, introduced in the early 1970's by Fenwick, are an example of a successful skimming approach. Penetration, in contrast, is used when many close substitutes make initial demand very elastic. Also, potentially large production economies may be envisioned if consumers can be convinced to buy. Numerous Internet start-ups are examples.

Multiproduct Pricing:
Equimarginalism Versus Loss Leaders

Suppose that rather than selling one product, a firm is selling many final products. Before you can decide on a coherent pricing policy, you must first determine which products are substitutes and which are complements.

If you are only selling goods that are *substitutes* for each other (consumers buy one or the other to satisfy a given desire), then you allocate much like the movie theater under third degree price discrimination. You must get the same net marginal gain from the last unit of good A sold as from the last unit of B, C, etc. Equimarginalism is the answer. If you are, instead, selling *complements* (goods consumed jointly) then and only then do you consider using *loss leaders*. Here certain products sold below their AC in order to induce purchases of a related product and markups across products vary greatly. Polaroid sells cameras at low prices in order to induce the sale of film, and shavers are practically given away at times to entice people to buy the companies razor blades.

Transfer Pricing of Inputs Within the Firm

For our final input pricing issue, suppose that a firm produces an input in one division that it uses in the production of its final product in another division. At which price does it "transfer" the intermediate product between divisions in order to maximize total company profits?

First and foremost, a price must be charged since the input has an opportunity cost. Transferring at a zero price causes a major misallocation of resources within the firm. With this in mind, we must see whether an external market exists for the input.

If no external market exists and the firm is producing this input strictly for its own use, then the transfer price should be the marginal costs of production. Under no conditions should firm-wide overhead be arbitrarily assigned to individual divisions and attempted to be captured through the transfer prices. Firm-wide overhead should only be assigned and captured on the sale of the final product (if the market permits). Otherwise efficiency and total profit maximization are foregone. Furthermore, company bonuses cannot be based solely on the returns of divisions since those providing the input won't show the returns of the final sales division.

Now suppose that an external market exists for the input in addition to the internal demand. The firm again considers opportunity cost. If the external market is competitive, then the opportunity cost of keeping the input is the competitive price it could have obtained. So this is what is charged internally. On the other hand, if the external market is monopolistic, then the opportunity cost of keeping the input is not the market price, but rather it is marginal revenue. The firm charges the outside market the monopoly price and charges marginal revenue internally. It doesn't use its monopoly power on itself. It's as Robert De Niro as Al Capone emphasized so emphatically, "We're a team, we're a team, we're a team!"

Concluding Remarks

The ideas in this chapter serve a number of critical purposes. The language and pictures of long-run equilibria for firms under various market structures is invaluable for the understanding of basic pricing behavior, delving into antitrust actions and reactions, and conveying why free-market economists love the dynamic mature of the marketplace in general.

Additionally, the simple single-product models can be extended to take into account new products, multiproducts, and transfer pricing within the firm. Elasticities of demand, marginal costs, and the number and reaction of rivals remain the key features throughout the analysis. Now that we're schooled in micro foundation, we're ready to make the transition to macroeconomic models and forecasting. Technical aspects come first, followed by the major macro schools of thought in Chapter Six.

Q: How can economists look at the same data on the economy and come up with such different views?
A: The same way that chefs can come up with so many different dishes from the same set of ingredients.
—Marilyn vos Savant

CHAPTER FIVE

THE TECHNICAL TRANSITION FROM MICROECONOMICS TO MACROECONOMICS

In moving from the domain of individual markets into the domain of the entire economy, technical concepts must be covered before any theoretical differences among economists can be addressed. The first section in this chapter deals with money. Just what is it really? How did it come about, and what functions does it perform? What was its history up to Adam Smith? What is its history in the U.S.? How is money defined today?

The second section relates to the measurement of wealth. Score must be kept on how well the economy is doing today compared to its past. The *Wealth of Nations* emphasized goods and services as national wealth, but how is final production measured in practical terms? And why is the difference between "real" and "nominal" values so important?

The third section goes into Say's Law and the inherent stability of a free-market economy at full employment. To avoid wasting productive labor, full employment is certainly a goal of macroeconomics. How is this defined? If an economy is at less than full employment, does this paradoxically mean that certain goods are being oversupplied? Are they produced but not sold because there is a lack of demand by the unemployed labor? How long can this overproduction and apparent waste continue?

The final section presents the Equation of Exchange, which brings together four basic macro variables together for a better understanding of an economy's dynamics. This conceptual framework has existed for centuries and combines the money and the real sides of the economy in a simple, direct way.

Money: It's Not the Root of All Evil

What is money? What "backs" it? And why is it often called the "lifeblood" of the marketplace? To answer these questions, let's start with a simple barter economy.

Barter is extremely inefficient. For exchange to take place, each party in the trade must have exactly what the other party desires. In other words, there must be a "double coincidence of wants". The search and transaction costs associated greatly hinder exchange.

The result is that eventually something will begin to circulate as a go-between. Whatever this money is, it serves as a *medium of exchange* that reduces search and transactions costs. It is extremely productive in this sense. Goods and services flow more smoothly. They are carried along by the "lifeblood" of the market.

The medium of exchange may be anything, and throughout history the list of items that have served as money is incredible. Ranging from wood and rocks to shells and beads to various metals to crops (like tobacco or rice) to cigarettes in prisoner of war camps to various animals to slaves to pieces of paper to accounts on a computer, the fact that stands out is that money is based on <u>extreme</u> <u>trust</u>. Someone else will want it from you.

There is an air of mystery and even myth about money. Coins in ancient times came out of the temples, minted by the priests, and why today the Fed and other central banks continue to operate behind elaborate, temple-like edifices and speak in deeply earnest, solemn tones. Too much is at stake for society's masses to run amok by not trusting the money supply. The *Bible* states that it is "for the *love* of money [that] is a root of all kinds of evil." On a purely social basis, abstract money is a wonderous mechanism if "well-managed."

Properties and Functions of Money

As a medium of exchange, society would like the go-between to have a number of desirable properties. Ideally, it is easy to recognize, hard to counterfeit or copy, quite durable, highly divisible (for making small change), and easy to carry.

After something begins to serve effectively as a medium of exchange, it automatically takes on two other functions. One is to serve as a *standard of value*. Rather than one horse being worth so many chickens, and so many chickens being worth so many sheep, all goods are translated into their single money price. A horse costs $2,000; a chicken costs $10.00, and so on for each good. Thinking about market value is made more economical.

The other function is to serve as a *store of value*. In this case, money (wages and salaries) from the present are postponed for future consumption. The store-of-value function brings inflation directly into the picture. Unanticipated inflation rewards debtors. In contrast, low inflation and sound money rewards savers, creditors, and fixed-income households. Typically, inflation redistributes resources from "ants" to "grasshoppers". No wonder sound-money economists believe that the fairest action any government can undertake for its people is to have zero inflation. If not, past work effort through saving is being penalized through devaluation of the money supply.

General History of Money to the Time of Adam Smith

Lumps or bars of silver and bronze were used as money as early as the second millennium before Christ. These metals are easy to recognize, hard to copy, quite durable, and highly divisible. Since rulers always wanted gold and silver, citizens had trust that someone would accept the metals in exchange from them.

Precious nuggets as first metal money required a set of scales for transactions. Coinage – bearing the device, stamp, or seal of a state – was invented in the 7th century B.C. Early coins were minted by priests in the temples. Croesus of Lydia, king from 560 to 546 B.C., is the first known ruler to issue gold and silver coins whose purity were guaranteed by the government.

Chapter 5

Coins simplified exchange since they were uniform in weight and stamped with an official seal to enhance acceptability. Originally there were *full-bodied* coins whose face value as money equaled the metal market value if melted down. So secondary opportunities always existed. To prevent the "clipping" of edges, full-bodied coins took on uniform, round shapes with grooved edges.

Extensive usage of full-bodied coins means that the quantity of money in use can fluctuate significantly as people swing back-and-forth from spending the coins to melting them down for plates, jewelry, and other needs. Also, strict adherence to full-bodied coins means that the sovereign or government gets no minting mark-up – no "seigniorage." Accordingly, along came *token* coins whose face value as money is greater than their metallic value. They are found in Greece as early as the Hellenistic period. Practically all coins in the world today are token.

As for paper money, the first officially issued exchange notes were Exchange Certificates in China in the 12th century AD. Private paper money evolved from people who stored their (full-bodied) coins with the local goldsmith and were given a receipt in return. This piece of paper was literally "as good as gold." It was *fully-backed* currency. Subsequently, the gold backing was reduced, as goldsmiths/banks began issuing receipts without 100 percent of the gold in reserve, thereby creating *fractionally-backed* currency. Ultimately all metallic backing was removed by governments so that paper currency became *fiat*, simply "legal tender" by political order.

The last step is even more incredible. The majority of the basic money supply in the U.S. and other countries is not fiat currency and token coins. Instead it is in the form of checking accounts (demand deposits), which are not backed by either metal or fiat. People accept your checks because they want to, not because they have to, and this type of money is managed through computers. Money has become increasingly abstract.

In Adam Smith's time, both full-bodied and token coins circulated. The British public typically hoarded the full-bodied coins in times of inflation, using the cheaper token coins for the most efficient medium of exchange. Paper money also circulated. The Bank of England was chartered in 1694, and it issued paper pound sterling notes backed by specie. In addition, private bank notes (paper receipts backed by goldsmiths and private bankers) and small denomination fiat paper currency circulated as well.

One of Smith's major concerns in the *Wealth of Nations* was the establishment of a private banking system that responded to growing commerce needs without the over-issuance of money. He felt that private banks were absolutely necessary in their role as *intermediaries*. Banks take the coins of people who want to save them or don't want to carry them around, then use them as reserves (held in the vault) against the private paper money that they create for transactional convenience and business loans. Merchants do not have to hold back gold and silver coins to cover unexpected payments and for large expenditures at certain times of the year. Instead, this capital (as Smith called it) could be placed in banks to earn interest, with bank loans then taken out to meet emergency or seasonal needs.

The Bank of England in Smith's day was not a central bank as we think of that institution presently. It didn't regulate commerce and seek price stability. Instead, it was established to be the main clearinghouse and leading banker for the government. The key objectives were to make the metallic standard function more efficiently and to meet the debt needs of the government. The Bank of England exchanged pound sterling for specie, held government accounts, and was instrumental in making orderly markets for issuing government bonds to finance wars and other public projects.

Smith favored a *real-bills doctrine*, where the creation of a bank loan or private paper currency is based on a "real bill of exchange". Since a real bill is a security that only results when the actual production/sale of real goods is imminent, banks only provide credit in response to new production coming into the market. Changes in the money supply are the endogenous consequences of real production rather than being exogeneously determined by the central bank. The growth in the money supply moves internally with the business cycle rather than externally determined by monetary authorities to offset real problems.

Critical Themes in the Monetary History of the U.S.

In the following monetary history of the U.S., four overarching themes are present. They are:

- **Constant struggle between the sound and easy money forces.** At issue here is a fundamental question in equity, and the rich-versus-downtrodden debate has often swirled around the extent and growth of the money supply.
- **Periodic panics.** From the time of the Revolutionary War through the first third of the 20th century, the U.S. experienced financial panics about every twenty years.
- **Tried everything.** The U.S. financial history is as complex as any nation in world history because we have tried just about everything imaginable as money at some point.
- **More abstract money.** The majority of the U.S. money exists today on computers in the form of accounts.

The U.S. from the 1650's to 1907

After using commodities like tobacco and rice – "country pay" – as money prior to the 1650's, the individual colonies began to mint their own coins. England ended the practice in the 1684. Next, the colonies began to bills of credit and paper money. By 1764, England had stopped that practice as well in all colonies. At the start of the Revolutionary War, the lack of paper money meant that token coins, many of which were foreign, were the primary medium-of-exchange in the colonies.

(1) American Revolution to the War of 1812

Faced with financing government expenditures in 1775, the Continental Congress issued paper currency called *continen-*

tals. First backed to some extent by Spanish silver dollars, continentals turned quickly into fiat currency. They became so worthless that Washington's soldiers stuffed them in boots to fill holes or burned them for heat. Most significantly, the U.S. as a republic was born with hyperinflation due to a flood of worthless paper money, and a common lament in the early years of the republic was, "It ain't worth a continental".

The runaway inflation galvanized the sound money forces, led by Alexander Hamilton as the first Secretary of the Treasury. Hamilton drew extensively upon Smith ideas about banking. Like Smith, he wanted a sound financial system regulated by more than just the free-market movement of specie from bank to bank. Hamilton wanted an institution similar to the Bank of England.

As proposed by Hamilton and his followers, the U.S. Constitution specifies quite clearly that Congress only has the power "to coin money and regulate the value thereof." Nothing more and nothing less is stated. Like Smith, Hamilton took for granted self-adjusting specie standard where gold and silver back paper money and loans. Consequently, the Constitution limited Congress' monetary role to setting the legal tender value of the metal used for coins, the primary medium-of-exchange at the time. Paper money was then to be issued by private state-chartered banks regulated through a national bank.

There were only four banks in the U.S. when Hamilton got his wish for the a national bank in 1791. The First Bank of the United States was chartered for 20 years to aid the government in attaining loans, to assist in the sale of public lands, and to hold revenues collected by the U.S. government. It strengthened U.S Treasury credit by using government debt as part of its capitalization. The First Bank accepted payments to the federal government in the form of private notes and currency, and it issued its own bills of credit. It kept the state banks in check by not accepting "bad" private notes.

The Coinage Act in 1792 put the U.S. legally on a bimetallic standard of gold and silver. The U.S. Treasury would, *with-*

out seignoriage, mint raw gold and silver into dollar coins with a specified amount of gold or silver content (15 ounces of silver were set to equal 1 ounce of gold). Therefore, citizens would always know what a gold or silver dollar is worth by law, and the government could not take advantage of the coin-creation process.

Large discoveries of silver in Virginia immediately after the passage of the Coinage Act caused the American public to hoard gold rather than spend it. This reflected *Gresham's Law,* in which "bad" money drives "good" money out circulation. Gold was the good money since it was undervalued at the mint—private citizens did not bring gold to the U.S. Treasury to be minted into coins—so only silver coins circulated. Moreover, the American public soon began to hoard U.S. silver dollars and spend Spanish silver dollars because of slight differences in metallic content. President Thomas Jefferson stopped the coinage of U.S. silver dollars as a result, and America once again used foreign coins as the primarily medium-of-exchange.

By 1811, 117 state-chartered banks were on the scene. The First Bank was not re-chartered that year. It was detested by those against centralization of federal power and despised by those who wanted easy money and credit. This combination was one that the sound money advocates could not stop at the time.

(2) 1812 to 1861: Times to Romp, Stomp and Romp Again
Just as the firm hand of the First Bank was removed from the U.S. economy, the War of 1812 broke out. Excessive issuance of U.S. Treasury notes to finance the war over the next three years led to the Panic of 1815. By 1816, the number of state banks had romped up to 232.

The Second Bank of the United States was chartered in 1816, again for twenty years, but with a far larger financial base than the First Bank. The Second Bank became a very important player in the economy when Nicholas Biddle became its third president in 1823. A member of the powerful Biddle family of Philadelphia, he possessed an aristocratic, imperialistic attitude and represented the sound-money establishment. Therefore, his immediate intent was to tighten regulation of the banking system by stomping on bad banks.

The election of 1828 saw Andrew Jackson, representing the common folk of farmers, small business owners, and westerners, as the Democratic candidate for president. He sharply criticized the Biddle's actions. After the election, Jackson threatened to close the Second Bank, and in the summer of 1832, he vetoed a recharter bill passed by the Biddle supporters in Congress. After his re-election in the fall, Jackson sent a strong message about his contempt for the Second Bank by removing U.S. government deposits from it and placing them in state banks.

The brewing recession in 1834 led the Jackson administration to devalue the gold dollar through the Gold Coin Act. The exchange ratio was changed to 16 ounces of silver per one ounce of gold in order to slightly overvalue gold at the mint and undervalue silver. The mint price of gold was set at $20.67 per ounce, making silver $1.29 per ounce, and this gold price will be maintained from 1834 to 1933 with the exception of the greenback period from 1861 to 1878. The net inflow of specie to the U.S. caused the money supply to grow over 40 percent and prices over 35 percent between 1834 and 1837.

A collapse of bank credit induced the panic of 1837 as the state-chartered banks lost specie (reserves) to the people and state governments. But net specie inflows continued to the U.S. in 1838, and banks soon resumed species payments. The lack of a national bank, combined with an intense desire by the states to be free of federal regulatory control, set off another romp in the 1840's and 1850's.

In came the era of "free banking" and "wildcat banking". Free banking meant that just about anyone wanting a state banking charter was able to obtain one. Even though states had laws about what constituted required reserves to be held against bank notes and loans/credit, the regulations were often loosely enforced. Home offices could be deep in the woods, making redemption of paper currency for specie next to impossible and creating so-called wildcat banks (out where the wildcats live).

Gold discoveries in California and Australia in the 1840's kept specie and credit abundant. Numerous types of private money circulated in the 1850's. The excess of paper currencies finally caused another Panic of 1857, in which foreign coins were then dropped as legal tender by Congress. At the start of the Civil War, 1,600 state banks existed, with some 7,000 different types of "legal" bank notes. Plus another 5,000 types of counterfeit notes were present since the printing press was readily available. The 1840's and 1850'5 were a money free-for-all.

(3) 1861 to 1907: National Banks, Deflation, and the Great Panic

In typical fashion, the Civil War led the Union government in 1861 to print fiat currency called *greenbacks* (because of their green ink), continuing until the end of 1863. High inflation was the predictable outcome. Even so, greenbacks were the first national paper currency of the U.S., remaining in circulation until the end of 1878.

The free-banking era in the U.S. came to a screeching halt at the end of 1863 when the Union government discovered a far more effective way to finance the war than with greenbacks. National banks would now be chartered by the U.S. Treasury, and they would fund much of the war effort through the purchase of special government bonds obtained with their national bank notes.

The National Banking Act of 1863 created the Office of the Comptroller of the Currency (OCC), within the Department of Treasury, to charter national banks. Careful scrutiny of officers and directors was implemented and sound capital requirements were established for national banks. Because only the national banks could buy the special government bonds, which earned interest directly, and because the bonds could also be used as reserves (like specie) for issuing loans, which earned even further interest, this was a great deal for the national banks. The plan worked like a dream to finance the war. Greenbacks were no longer printed after 1863.

In 1865, Congress levied a 10% tax on all new state bank notes as a further move toward sound money. The number of state-chartered banks plummeted from nearly 1,400 in 1865 to less than 250 by 1873. More financial tightening occurred in 1873 when Congress decided that the U.S. government would no longer mint silver dollars. Most of Europe had adopted a classic gold standard starting in 1867, and the U.S. government wanted to move in this direction as well. Little debate took place at the time of passage in 1873, and the Panic of 1873 ensued.

In 1875, Congress decided to redeem greenbacks for gold four years hence on January 1, 1879. As a result, the U.S. went onto a *de facto* gold standard in 1879, even though the bimetallic standard was still legally in effect. The official U.S. price of gold returned to $20.67 per ounce.

During the last third of the 19th century, deflation occurred. U.S. producer and consumer prices fell on average 1-2% per year. As expected, the easy-money crowd of populists, farmers, and small business owners screamed foul. The dropping of silver dollars in 1973 caused them to rebrand it the CRIME OF 1873. Great populist gatherings took place on the plains and worker riots occurred in the cities throughout the 1880's.

Financial panics arose in 1890 and 1893 over the uncertain role of silver in official U.S. financial affairs. The 1896 Republic platform under William McKinley called for a legal gold standard, while the Democrat platform under William Jennings Bryan called for a bimetallic standard with an equal role for both silver and gold. Even though Bryan pleaded, "do not crucify mankind on a cross of gold", the Democrats lost, and large gold discoveries in Alaska and South Africa soon thereafter ended any hope for the silver forces. In 1900, a *full gold standard* was legally adopted through the Gold Standard Act (more properly the Currency Act).

Chapter 5

A full gold standard meant that the U.S. government was now prepared to buy and sell gold at a fixed price to *anyone*. Gold was to flow freely in and out of the country at the fixed price of $20.67 an ounce for paper notes issued by the U.S. Treasury. Private state and national banks also issued their own paper currencies backed by gold or gold-dominated reserves in the early 1900's. The number of banks increased significantly as gold flowed into the U.S. from the rest of the world. Reserves were highly leveraged throughout the U.S. banking industry.

Then wham! The Great Panic of 1907 hits the country. It exposed the basic weaknesses of the U.S. banking system. Not enough gold existed to pay off the fractionally-backed currency, and there was no legal lender of last resort. It was a private citizen, J.P. Morgan, who stepped forward as the lender of last resort in 1907. He promised to loan his personal gold supply to the U.S. government to avert more bank runs. The panic stopped. And so, in the name of self-fulfilling prophecies, did the further usage of the word "panic" to describe "depressions" or "downturns". It was time for a national lender of last resort.

The Creation of the Federal Reserve System in 1913 and Subsequent Modifications

The Federal Reserve System was created in 1913 to avoid major financial crises. Modeled along the Smith-Hamilton lines of a bank that facilitated trade rather than one that pursued specific macroeconomic objectives like zero inflation, the "Fed" was to be the U.S. government's lender of last resort. In the process, the Fed was to make the gold standard function more smoothly and to furnish an elastic currency that responded quickly to financing needs of the economy. It was to be a banker's bank. Summary points about the Fed include:

- There are 12 Federal Reserve banks (districts) rather than one central bank. The original intent was to diversify power. Each district Fed has its own President elected by the member banks in the district.

- The Fed was set up to be an "independent" agency. In other words, even though the President nominates the Chair of the Fed and other Board members, who are then approved by Congress, and even though the Chair of the Fed periodically testifies before Congress, the Fed's monetary actions are free of direct control by the Executive or Legislative branches of government. The Fed is a "quasi" government agency.
- One tool of the Fed is the *discount rate*, the interest rate the district Fed banks charge member banks to borrow additional reserves. An increase in the discount rate indicates monetary tightening, while a decrease indicates monetary easing. The discount rate is often changed in conjecture with the federal funds rate.
- A second closely related tool is the *federal funds rate*, an extremely short-term (24-hour) interest rate at which banks loan and borrow excess reserves. The Fed strongly influences this rate, where again a rise means monetary tightening and a decline means easing. Unlike the discount rate, this rate fluctuates day-to-day around its targeted value.
- A third tool is setting *reserve requirements*. Banks must hold a specified percentage of their demand deposits and other checkable accounts in the form of reserves (by Fed definition today either coins/currency in the vault or a bank's deposit account at the Fed, neither of which earn interest). An increase in the reserve requirement indicates monetary tightening and a decrease indicates easier monetary policy. The Fed rarely changes reserve requirements because it has such a big effect on the banking system and its profitability.
- Since 1935, the most frequently-used tool of the Fed to affect the day-to-day money supply is to conduct *open market operations*. The Fed buys and sells government securities. *Buying* government securities means the Fed

is *easing* – the Fed is injecting money into the economy and removing government securities. In contrast, *selling* government securities the Fed is *tightening*.

• The original discount policy required the 12 Federal Reserve Banks to "confine [discounts] to short-term, self-liquidating paper growing out of actual commercial, industrial and agricultural operations, in the restrictive senses of the terms, and ... particular care [should] be taken not to discount or purchase paper which had been issued for the purpose of providing capital investment for any business." In other words, the real-bills doctrine was in force. The 12 Fed banks were anticipated to exert prime influence on the creation of credit in their own districts at the time the Federal Reserve System was established. The changed with the Banking Act of 1935.

• The 12 Federal Reserve banks are "owned" by their member banks who purchase stock in them. All national banks are members of the Federal Reserve System, and state banks have their choice to be members.

• Originally, the Federal Reserves banks were required to keep at least 40 percent of Federal Reserve notes and at least 35 percent of member bank deposits in gold reserves. This is no longer the case. All gold backing was removed in 1968.

• The main administrative body overseeing the Fed system is the seven-person Board of Governors. Each is nominated by the president, approved by Congress, and serves a non-renewable 14-year term. One of the seven Board of Governors is the Chair of the Fed. Until the Banking Act of 1935, the U.S. Secretary of the Treasury was an ex officio member of the Board and served as Chair of the Fed. Table 4.1 includes the Chairs of the Fed up to the time of writing.

• The group now responsible for setting U.S. monetary policy is the twelve-person Federal Open Market Committee

– the FOMC – consisting of the Board of Governors plus five voting district Presidents (rotating except that the New York President is always a voting member). The shift in responsibility for monetary policy from the district Feds and discount policy (as envisioned in 1913) to the Board, the FOMC and open-market policy occurred through the Banking Act of 1935.

Table 5.1: Chairs of the Fed

Dates Served	Name
Aug. 10, 1914-Aug. 9, 1916	Charles S. Hamlin
Aug.10, 1916-Aug. 9, 1922	W.P.G. Harding
May 1, 1923-Sept. 15, 1927	Daniel R. Crissinger
Oct. 4, 1927- Aug. 31, 1930	Roy A. Young
Sept. 16, 1930-May 10,1933	Eugene Meyer
May 19, 1933-Aut. 15, 1934	Eugene R. Black
Nov. 15, 1934-Jan. 31, 1948	Marriner S. Eccles
Apr.15, 1948-Mar. 31, 1951	Thomas B. McCabe
Apr. 2, 1951-Jan. 31, 1970	Wm. McChesney Martin, Jr.
Feb. 1, 1970-Jan. 31, 1978	Arthur F. Burns
Mar. 8, 1978-Aug. 6, 1979	G. William Miller
Aug. 6, 1979-Aug.11, 1987	Paul A. Volcker
Aug. 11, 1987-Present	Alan Greenspan

U.S. Monetary History: 1914 to the Present

When World War I broke out in Europe in 1914, the U.S. remained on a full gold standard even though the European countries abandoned it. They were unwilling to pay gold bullion for their paper currencies to anyone and allow it to flow freely across their borders.

At the end of the war in 1919, 30,000 banks stretched across the U.S. landscape. Since European countries had abandoned the gold standard, and since no powerful international clearinghouse arose, along came a period of unorganized exchange rates. It would last until 1944 and the Bretton Woods agreements. The Roaring Twenties saw Americans turning inward. The brutality of a world war and the European financial problems immediately thereafter generated a feeling of U.S. isolationism. It was a time to enjoy the fruits of scientific progress as the quality of life changed drastically with electricity, cars, radios, and other innovations prior to 1929.

(1) The Crash of 1929 through Bretton Woods and World War II

The October 1929 stock market crash brought the Roaring Twenties to an abrupt end. The Fed believed the crash resulted from excessive liquidity in the economy. While the money supply growth in M_2 was quite low from 1926 onward (less than four percent each year from 1926 to 1929), the Fed chose to raise interest rates and shrink the money supply after the crash. Incredibly, from the end of 1929 to 1933, M_2 *declined* nearly a third! Both the Fed and Treasury hoarded gold rather than acting as a true lenders of last resort prepared to sell every last ounce of gold to defend the paper currency.

Since money is the lifeblood of the market, the Fed, in conjunction with the Treasury, bled the system excessively. Of the nearly 31,000 banks that existed at the start of 1930, 30 percent had closed their doors by 1933. Four thousand went under in 1933 alone, with over 90 percent being one-office, small-town banks. The Fed failed miserably in every one of its objectives: as a lender of last resort, as a facilitator of the gold standard, and as a furnisher of an elastic currency.

Franklin Roosevelt, upon taking office in March, 1933, immediately declared an eight-day bank holiday. The American public was shell-shocked. As is typical in panic situations, Congress called special hearings and searched for a national scapegoat. The big banks were the obvious choice. The most famous banker of the day, Charles Mitchell of Chase, was ridiculed before Congress. The public outrage swept in a series of banking reforms.

The U.S. abandoned the full gold standard in 1933 through the Joint Resolution on the Discontinuance of Gold Payments.

The 1934 Gold Reserve Act substituted a *gold bullion standard* for the full gold standard. No longer could private citizens exchange U.S. paper dollars for gold – that privilege was reserved only for governments. For that matter, no longer could Americans own gold. All gold was called in by the government for Federal Reserve notes in 1934 at 20.67 per ounce, and it was now illegal to personally have more than small amounts of gold. Quickly thereafter the legal price of gold moved to $35.00 per ounce.

The Banking Act of 1933, with its Glass-Steagall provisions, created firewalls in the financial sector. Rather than financial supermarkets, three distinct financial institutions were now legally defined: commercial banks, investment banks, and savings and loan associations. Each would serve a particular market segment. Commercial banks would make commercial loans and trade government securities to generate profits, and no ownership or equity in private firms was permitted. Investment banks would underwrite securities. And savings and loans companies (S&L's) would concentrate on mortgage and real-estate loans. Overall, Glass-Steagall was a victory for small banks, in particular community banks.

The Federal Deposit Insurance Corporation (FDIC) also came into existence through the Banking Act of in 1933. Deemed to be the true lender of last resort for the U.S. economy, it immediately brought bank failures to a halt. Only nine banks went under in 1934, and by 1940 the number of U.S. banks had stabilized at 15,000. From 1940 to 1980, an average of just six banks a year failed.

Finally, the Banking Act of 1933 specified a new form of price control. Interest on demand deposits was prohibited entirely, and the Federal Reserve Board was given the authority to set interest rate ceilings on saving and time deposits in banks and S&L's. Known as Regulation Q, these interest rate ceilings remained in effect until 1980.

In 1934 Roosevelt appointed Marriner Eccles as acting Secretary of the Treasury and Chair of the Fed. Eccles was strongly in favor of expansionary fiscal policy to offset the Great Contraction of 1932-33. He willingly subjugated Fed monetary policy to the wishes of the U.S. Treasury to keep interest rates low on government securities in order to reduce financing costs on deficits and national debt.

With strong support from Eccles, the Banking Act of 1935 was passed. As noted earlier, the Board of Governors was now given prime control of U.S. money policy, centralizing power away from the 12 district Feds. Open-market operations in U.S. government securities, rather than the discounting of bank paper at district Feds, became the major tool affecting the expansion or contraction of the U.S. money supply. Since everyone agreed that government securities are not real bills, the real-bills doctrine fell by the wayside.

Open-market operations would, henceforth, be conducted by the FOMC, comprised of the seven Board of Governors plus five (rotating) district Fed Presidents. This was a compromise to those wanting Board control, but not total power, in Washington D.C. The Chair of the Fed would now be an appointed member of the Board of Governors rather than the ex officio Secretary of the Treasury.

In 1936 and 1937, in a truly astonishing move, the Fed raised reserve requirements. It was anticipating inflation! This hammered already depressed banking conditions and killed the incipient recovery under way. Monetary policy was in shambles.

When World War II broke out, the Fed continued with a low interest rate policy in order to help the U.S. Treasury finance the war at the lowest costs possible. However, even with the sale of war bonds that generated huge government revenues and soaked up possible consumption spending, and even with extensive price controls from 1942 onward, inflation raged. Coupons, long lines, and black markets were commonplace as money growth shot through the roof. M_2 growth averaged 15+ percent a year from 1942 through 1945.

In 1944, the allies came together in the famous Bretton Woods meetings in New Hampshire. The grand intent was to restructure the international financial structure to create greater exchange rate stability. The principles architects were Harry Dexter White, Undersecretary of the U.S. Treasury, and John Maynard Keynes, the British government's leading representative. The signed agreement called for an international gold bullion standard in which currencies were to be valued in gold or U.S. dollars valued at $35.00 per ounce of gold.

Since all currencies were defined per ounce of gold or the U.S. dollar, a fixed exchange- rate system was locked in place. The newly-established International Monetary Fund (IMF) would henceforth serve as the worldwide clearinghouse for currencies. It would help member countries overcome short-term foreign exchange shortages and address more persistent exchange rate problems. The new World Bank would assist in development loans by channeling money from wealthier countries to poorer parts of the world. Free trade and openness rather than tariffs and isolationism would be the new world order.

(2) 1946 to the Present: Regulation Versus Deregulation

U.S. financial markets were tightly regulated throughout the 1940's and 1950's. The Glass-Steagall firewalls segmented financial firms, price ceilings existed on demand and time deposits, interstate banking was prohibited, and so as was branch banking in many states. National banks were examined by three separate national agencies: the Fed, the Comptroller of the Currency, and the FDIC.

In 1951, the Fed and the U.S. Treasury reached their historic Accord. No longer would the Fed be subservient to the Treasury's demands for "orderly" security markets and low interest rates. Instead, the Fed would henceforth conduct monetary policy "independently".

William M. Martin, Jr. was appointed Chair of the Fed in 1951 (after having been the youngest president of the New York Stock Exchange). He undertook sound monetary policy throughout the 1950's: money supply (M_2) growth averaged less than 4 percent per year form 1950 to 1960. Martin said the Fed "must take the punch bowl away once the party gets started" and "must lean against the wind." Very few bank failures resulted in the 1950's, and people joked about "banker's hours".

Martin began to lose his grip on sound money starting in 1961. Then the Viet Nam War gave rise to deficit spending at the same time of Johnson's Great Society. The Fed "monetized" deficits through open-market purchases in 1967-68 and the quantity of U.S. dollars in the world exploded. This led to the elimination of the gold backing of Federal Reserve notes in 1968. Easy, easy money was the order of the day.

President Nixon closed the gold window to the rest of the world in 1971. The U.S. stopped redeeming federal reserve notes for gold and replaced the Bretton Woods system of fixed exchange rates with floating rates. At the same time, national wage and price controls were implemented. By 1973, the market price of gold was $140 an ounce. Nominal interest rates, significantly higher than the early sixties, were putting tremendous pressure on commercial banks and savings and loan companies (S&L's). The interest rate ceilings on demand and time deposits allowed brokerage houses, credit unions, and money stores to take away conventional banking markets. Money market mutual funds burst on the scene. Plus banks faced growing pressure and legislation to be more community and socially-minded in their lending policies.

Major deregulation came in 1980 through the Monetary Reform Act and Depository Institutions Deregulations Act. Interest rate ceilings were phased out and more competition began across traditional firewalls. S&L's undertook much more aggressive lending tactics. The S&L industry became a moral hazard by the mid-1980's, ultimately leading to the establishment of the Resolution Trust Corporation (RTC) in 1989 to sell off the bad debts as quickly as possible. Pressure continued to mount for expanded interstate banking and further removal of the vestiges of Glass-Steagall.

Alan Greenspan was appointed Chair of the Fed in August, 1987. He has turned out to be the savior of the banking industry and stock markets up to this point. Contrary to the expectations that the banking industry might go the way of the S&L's industry in the early 1990's and necessitate extensive bailouts, the industry has enjoyed record profitability. The FOMC, through Greenspan, is known for activist monetary approach. It takes preemptive strikes against inflation. It is a major force in international markets. A real-bills doctrine or a full gold standard both seem implausible at the moment (even Greenspan in the past has forcefully defended the merits of a gold standard).

Interstate banking and branching became legal June 1, 1997. Traditional firewalls continue to weaken as financial institutions merge. Even so, small, community banks remain very much on the landscape. Slightly over 9,000 banking organizations (holding companies, independent commercial banks, thrifts) exist in the U.S. today, and Glass-Steagall still has not been totally repealed after numerous attempts.

In the aftermath of the 1980 "deregulation", the banking system is now regulated by the Fed, the OCC, the FDIC, 50 state bank supervisors, the Justice Department, the SEC, the Treasury Department, and the Federal Home Loan Bank Board. What red tape and a regulatory nightmare, especially for smaller banks! The following points summarize major U.S. banking legislation and actions sequentially since 1951:

- The Fed-Treasury Accord of 1951.
- The 1956 Banking Holding Act (Douglas amendment) that rejected interstate bank expansion.
- The Smithsonian Agreement in 1971, in which all remnants of the gold standard were abandoned.
- U.S. citizens allowed to own gold in 1975.
- The Community Reinvestment Act of 1977 that required banks to make loans to meet community needs and to

make mortgage and other loans primarily where deposits originate. This was a determined attempt to make banks more socially responsible.

- The Humphrey-Hawkins Act of 1978 that required the Fed to periodically report to Congress how it's doing with regard to unemployment, inflation, and output growth.
- The Monetary Reform Act of 1980, landmark legislation that gave the Fed the power to set reserve requirements for all depository institutions, established NOW accounts, and permitted more financial competition.
- The Depository Institutions Deregulations Act of 1980 that phased out all interest rate ceilings over the next six years.
- The St. Germain-Garn Act of 1982 that encouraged S&L's to make more risky loans, creating a classic moral hazard situation.
- The Basil Accords of 1988 that set international capital standards for banks.
- The Financial Institutions Reform, Recovery and Enforcement Act (FIRREA) of 1989 to resolve the S&L crises through the Resolution Trust Corporation. Also referred to as the *"Frankly, I'm a Rich Real Estate Appraiser"* Act.
- The FDIC Improvement Act of 1992 that restructured the deposit insurance fund for banks and thrifts.
- The Riegle-Neil Interstate Banking and Branching Efficiency Act of 1994 that allowed banks to merge across state line starting June 1, 1997.

Definitions of U.S. Monetary Aggregates

Although economists talk about "the" U.S. money supply, there are actually a series of different concepts of money. To be absolutely precise, these are money "stocks" rather than flows. The most liquid of all money is currency (paper money and coins) because of its ease in converting to goods and services. Financial assets with less liquidity then enter the picture. Let's start with the most basic concept of the U.S. money stock, namely M_1, and then build upon it. Keep in mind the ongoing abstraction of money.

- M_1: the sum of currency held outside the vaults of depository institutions, Federal Reserve Banks, and the U.S. Treasury; *plus* travelers checks; *plus* demand and other checkable deposits issued by financial institutions (except demand deposits due to the Treasury and depository institutions); *minus* cash items in the process of collection (checks being cleared) and Federal Reserve float. At the end of March, 2000, M_1 was approximately 1.1 trillion dollars, of which total checkable deposits comprised 53 percent and currency comprised 47 percent.

- M_2: M_1 *plus* savings deposits (the sum of money market deposit accounts, and passbook and statement savings); *plus* small denomination (less than $100,000) time deposits issued by financial institutions; *plus* shares in retail money market mutual funds (funds with initial investments of less than $50,000); *net* of retirement accounts. At the end of March, 2000, M_2 was approximately 4.7 trillion dollars, of which savings/small time deposits comprised 58 percent and large time deposits/ retail money funds comprised 34 percent.

- M_3: M_2 *plus* large denomination ($100,000 or more) time deposits; *plus* repurchase agreements issued by depository institutions; *plus* Eurodollar deposits, specifically, dollar-denominated deposits due to nonbank U.S. addresses held at foreign offices of U.S. banks worldwide and all banking offices in Canada and the United Kingdom; *plus* institutional money market mutual funds (funds with initial investments of $50,000 or more).

- *MZM*: also known as "money zero maturity", is equal to M_2 *minus* small denomination time deposits *plus* institutional money market mutual funds (which are included in the non-M_2 component). It is similar to M_2 and was approximately 4.4 trillion dollars at the end of March, 2000.

- **L:** M_3 *plus* U.S. savings bonds; *plus* short-term Treasury securities; *plus* commercial paper *plus* bankers acceptances held by households and by firms other than depository institutions *plus* money market mutual funds

Typically M_1, or M_2, or MZM are used in economic forecasting. As we will see, Milton Friedman's monetarism prefers M_2 when assessing the economy, and M_2 will receive considerable attention in later chapters. M_3, and L get far less attention from most economists, much less from the American public, than M_1, M_2, or MZM.

In addition to these measures of money stocks, two other monetary aggregates are noteworthy. The first is *legal reserves*, the amount that the Fed requires a member bank to hold back against the creation of demand deposits (recall that gold and silver once served as reserves for banks). The other is the *monetary base*, what serves as the foundation for the creation of money by commercial banks.

- **(Adjusted) Legal Reserves:** the sum of vault cash *plus* the Federal Reserve Bank deposits held by depository institutions, with an adjustment for the effects of changes for statutory reserve requirements on the quantity of base money held by depositories. At the end of March, 2000, adjusted reserves were 65 billion dollars.
- **(Adjusted) Monetary Base:** the sum of currency in circulation outside Federal Reserve Banks and the U.S. Treasury (i.e., currency held by the public and in bank vaults) *plus* deposits of depository financial institutions at Federal Reserve Banks, with an adjustment of the effects of changes in statutory reserve requirements on the quantity of base money held by depositories. At the end of March, 2000, the monetary base was 585 *billion* dollars.

No one ever said that understanding the various money measures and concepts would be easy. But you can now appreciate areas of disagreement among macroeconomists. One measure of money works well in some forecasting circumstances, while another works far better under different assumptions and circumstances. Where should the line be drawn between monies and near-monies? The debates will never stop.

Measuring the Flows of Output and Income: The National Product Accounts

With the arrival of the Great Depression, 20th century economists realized how little they knew about the flows of production and national income. Some scholars even argue that a major reason for the U.S. economy plunging downward so sharply after the 1929 stock market crash was lack of data indicating just how serious things had become. In response, the 1930's saw the creation of the national income and product accounts, spearheaded in the U.S. by eventual Nobel laureate Simon Kuznets, and driven by the idea of consumer sovereignty.

The underlying concept here is quite simple. Just as businesses have an accounting balance sheet, with the two sides being assets and of liabilities whose totals must be equal at the end of the accounting period, the economy has a giant T-account whose two totals must also balance at the end of the year. National product accounts give Adam Smith's notion of wealth concrete form and provide a scorecard on the critical flows of the macroeconomy.

The Definitions of GNP and GDP

The *gross product* of a country is defined as the market value of all newly produced final goods and services (that are not resold) during some time period (for example, a year). Gross *national* product (GNP) is the market value of all such final goods and services produced by a country's permanent residents, including those overseas. Gross *domestic* product (GDP) is the market value of all final goods produced within a country's borders. These definition of GDP and GNP:

- stress *market value*, meaning that for the most part, only the goods and services that are traded in formal

markets and have a market price are included (house-wives services are not included for this reason);
- focus on **production**, not consumption or sales, meaning that increases in new inventory are included;
- emphasize **final** goods and services, those at the end of the production chain ready for consumption, not "intermediate goods" (like the wood used to make furniture);
- include the phrase **not resold** to avoid any double counting, and
- are stated per **time period**, meaning that GNP and GDP are flow (not stock) variables.

The economy's giant T-account measures GDP or GNP in two ways. One is to look at who is buying the final goods and services. This EXPENDITURE approach considers WHERE THE REVENUE IS COMING FROM. The other approach is to look at who is producing the final goods and services. This is the INCOME approach, which considers WHERE THE MONEY IS GOING TO.

The Expenditure Approach: C+I+G+(X-M)
The expenditure approach divides the demand for final goods and services (total spending) into four categories:
- **Consumption (C):** spending by households, which is further broken down into expenditures on durable goods (goods lasting three or more years like appliances and cars), on non-durable goods (food, clothing), and on services (haircuts, doctor visits).
- **Gross private domestic investment (I):** spending by private firms (the government has its own category), domestic in nature (foreign spending has its own category), and gross (rather than net) investment because depreciation is not subtracted out even though it is an intermediate product. The investment categories here are: new business plant and equipment, changes in inventory,

and new residential construction (yes, housing is defined as investment rather than durable-good consumption).

- *Government purchases (G):* strictly the purchase of goods and services by the government, not all government spending. Transfer payments (welfare spending, unemployment insurance) are not considered as final production.

- *Net foreign purchases (X-M):* exports (X), representing national production, are added in, whereas imports (M) are subtracted from GDP.

According to the *2000 Economic Report of the President*, nominal GDP in 1999 was provisionally $9.2 trillion, with C=$6.3 trillion (67%), I=$1.6 trillion (17%), G=$1.6 trillion (17%) and (x-m)= $-3 trillion (-3%)

The Income Approach: $W+R+i+\pi+CCA+IBT$

Turning to where a dollar of money goes to, the vast majority is in the form of *national income* (NY). A relatively small amount then goes to cover depreciation of equipment, or what is termed the *capital-consumption allowance* (CCA), with the rest going to the government in the form of *indirect business taxes* (IBT). Sales and excise taxes are IBT because they are levied *indirectly* on goods and services, whereas *direct taxes* like personal income taxes and corporate profit taxes are levied *directly* on people or firms and are already included in NY. GDP from the income side equals:

- *National income (NY):* national income is an *earnings* concept and is broken into four sub-categories: gross wages and salaries including salary supplements and proprietors' income (W); rental income (R); net interest income by private suppliers of financial capital (i); and corporate profits (), which consist of dividend payments, retained earnings, and corporate profits taxes.

- *Capital consumption allowance (CCA):* firms and the government hold back some of the money earned to cover the depreciation costs of plant and equipment. This "capital consumption allowance" is estimated by various accounting formulas rather than by the actual change in the market value of the asset as economists would prefer.

- ***Indirect business taxes (IBT):*** direct taxes such as income and corporate profits taxes are already included NY, but sales and excise taxes are not and must be taken separately into account.

According to the *2000 Economic Report of the President*, nominal GDP in 1999 from the income side was once again $9.2 trillion. NY equals some 80% of GDP, CCA equals 13%, and IBT equal 7%.

Alternative Measures of a Nation's Welfare beyond GDP
While GDP is the most widely reported measure of national welfare, the national product accounts furnish other measures of the well-being of the economy. Let's quickly review them since they frequently pop up in key economic forecasts or on the evening news.

GDP is supposedly a measure of the production of final goods and services, yet the depreciation of capital equipment is clearly an intermediate good. The reason capital depreciation is included in GDP is for practicality: calculating depreciation in precise market-value terms (the dollar loss in market value) is far too time consuming. Accounting estimates based on various formulas (e.g., straight-line depreciation, accelerated depreciation) are used instead. The total of the estimates is the capital consumption allowance (CCA). GDP minus CCA equals ***net domestic product*** (NDP). Some economists believe NDP is a better estimate of *final* production than GDP, even with the accounting difficulties, because a large intermediate component has been removed.

After indirect business taxes (IBT) are subtracted from NDP, the result is ***national income*** (NY). NY is an *earnings* concept rather than a *production* concept. It shows how much households and forms actually earn in the course of production after depreciation and indirect business taxes are subtracted from the money derived by firms from final production.

To get to how much households actually *receive* rather than earn requires further subtractions and additions. Social security contributions (FICA), corporate profits taxes, and retained earnings by corporations must be subtracted out, then government transfer payments (welfare, social security) must be added in. The result is *personal income* (PY), a *receipts* concept rather an earnings concept. After personal income taxes are subtracted from PY, the result is *disposable income* (DY), a further adjusted *receipts* concept. Most fundamentally, DY can be either consumed (C) or saved (S).

To summarize these discussions:

	GDP (Gross domestic product)
−	CCA (Capital consumption allowance)
=	NDP (Net domestic product)
−	IBT (indirect business taxes)
=	NY (W+R+i+π) (National income)
−	FICA, corporate profits taxes, retained earnings
+	Government transfer payments
=	PY (Personal income)
−	Personal income taxes
=	DY (Disposable income)
=	C+S

For the U.S. in 1999, nominal disposable income was $6.6 trillion (70% of GDP), of which $.2 trillion was saved and $6.4 trillion was consumed. Per capita nominal DY in the U.S. in 1999 totaled $24,000.

Nominal Versus Real GDP

Nominal GDP is GDP measured in current dollars. The current (average) price of each final good or service is multiplied by the amount produced, then all values are summed together: GDP= Σpq. The fundamental macro objective is to produce more total output as measured by the individual q's.

Individual prices (the p's) are necessary because they show the relative weights that society is valuing each q. A higher price indicates that society places more "value" on a good or service, whereas a lower price indicates less "value". From year to year, as more of some goods and less of others are produced, the price weights help determine if total production has increased or decreased.

The problem is that the absolute level of prices increases as inflation sets into the economy. Accordingly, nominal GDP may increase from one year to the next without any more of the actual or *real* q's being produced. The wealth of the nation is not growing, just prices are going up ($\Sigma p \overset{\uparrow}{q}$). In order to eliminate the effects of inflation, **nominal** GDP must be converted instead to GDP. This is done using the GDP deflator, a price index capturing all the goods and services that comprise GDP. Like the Consumer Price Index (CPI), the Wholesale Price Index (WPI), or the Producer Price Index (PPI), the GDP deflator is assigned a value of 100% (1.00) in its base year. At present, the GDP deflator base year is 1996. By dividing nominal GDP in 1999 by the GDP deflator, real GDP (with 1996 as the base year) was $8.9 trillion rather $9.2 trillion. The purely inflationary effects have been "divided out" to get to real output. Prices have been held constant from the base year ($\Sigma \overline{p} \overset{\uparrow}{q}$).

An inability to distinguish real values from nominal values is termed *money illusion.* Rising nominal money wages can cause the belief that welfare has improved even of the price index has risen by the same amount, and real wages remain the same. How much individuals can be tricked by money illusion is a crucial issue in the macroeconomic debates in the next chapter.

The Inherent Stability of Capitalism at Full Employment and Say's Law

Another critical issue in macroeconomic debates concerns the inherent stability of capitalism at full employment of the labor force. Before we address the issue, we must first define the labor force and full employment.

The U.S. Labor Force and Definitions of Unemployment

Not all adults are included in the official U.S. labor force. According to the U.S. Bureau of Labor Statistics, the labor force includes only those people either currently working or those actively seeking work if not employed. Those who do not wish to work are not part of the official labor force, nor are those who have given up looking, so-called *discouraged workers*.

What macroeconomics wants to avoid is *involuntary (cyclical)* unemployment. There will always be *frictional* unemployment (workers moving from one job to another) and *structural* unemployment (workers losing employment due to structural changes in the ways goods are produced). Consequently, full employment is never defined as 100 percent of the existing labor force working. Instead, in the U.S. the "acceptable" level of unemployment has hovered between 4 to 6 percent the past four decades, making full employment 94-96 percent of the labor force actually working.

Say's Law of Markets: Early Advocates and Major Critics

In terms of the inherent stability of capitalism at full employment, let's start with a simple barter economy. A worker only produces a product in order to immediately acquire other goods. Involuntary unemployment is never a problem, and the economy is always at full employment in the sense that those who want to work will find work.

What about for a monetary economy? Now when goods and services are produced, workers are paid money wages. Households in total may immediately turn around and buy all the goods and services being produced with the income being received, so that anything produced is sold and full employment of labor prevails. However, households in total may decide to save part of their incomes. This causes inventories to accumulate as final sales fall, generating more unemployment and "surplus" supplies of labor.

The key issue here is: can *prolonged* oversaving really occur in free-market economies? Can an overabundance of goods build up on the shelves, making surplus supplies of labor commonplace? Adam Smith, his devoted French disciple Jean-Baptiste Say, and British admirer David Ricardo both said no. The *Wealth of Nations* clearly rejected prolonged oversaving: "What is annually saved is as regularly consumed as what is annually spent, and nearly in the same time too; but it is consumed by a different set of people." Smith surmised that: "A man must be perfectly crazy who, where there is tolerable security, does not employ all the stock which he commands, whether he has own or borrowed of other people".

Say, in *Traité d'Economie Politique* (1803), formulated his famous Law of Markets. Expressed succinctly by Keynes as *supply creates its own demand*, Say's Law argue that there will never be a general glut of commodities in a scarce world: "It is production which opens a demand for products... Sales cannot said to be dull, because money is scarce, but because other products are so_ a product is no sooner created, than it, from that instant, affords a market for other products to the full extent of its own value".

Ricardo, in *Principles of Political Economy and Taxation* (1817), concurred: "Too much of a particular commodity may be produced, of which there may be such a glut in the market, as not to repay the capital expended on it; but thus cannot be the case with respect to all commodities." Reversals in full employment are temporary and are offset rather quickly by capital flows from the industries with surplus inventories to more prosperous investments.

Famous critics of Say's Law include Thomas Malthus, Karl Marx and John Maynard Keynes. These "liberal" economists believe that *too many workers are the fundamental problem in capitalistic economies*, creating prolonged periods of time when goods accumulate on sellers' shelves. The emphasis must be on equity rather than efficiency, as we will see in the classification of macroeconomic schools of thought from left to right in the next chapter. What might governments do to make the economy more "fair" in the face of persistent involuntary unemployment? Will central planning/industrializing policy be necessary to push the economy towards full employment? Are micro/macro conflicts inevitable?

The Equation of Exchange

The Equation of Exchange is simple, direct way of envisioning the interplay between the money and real sides of a macro economy. The equation has been around for centuries and is often associated with Adam Smith's friend David Hume. In its most widely recognized form, the Equation of Exchange is expressed as:

$$MV = PQ, \text{ where}$$

M= the money stock (M_2),

V= the velocity of the money stock — how often, on average, it changes hands or "turns over" in a year,

P= an absolute price index (the GDP deflator), and

Q= real output (real GDP).

The stock of money is multiplied by how fast it turns over gives the flow of total spending in the course of a year. The GDP deflator times real GDP gives nominal GDP, the flow of total production in the course of a year. Since the flow of total spending in current dollars must equal the flow of final production in current dollars, MV must equal PQ at the end of the year. To guarantee this is so, the velocity of the money stock is calculated last and is the balancing item in the equation.

The *velocity of money* is a critical variable in macro debates. *It is the inverse of the demand for money.* The *demand for money* (k) indicates why households and firms want to hold on to money (have it in their pockets or in bank accounts) rather than pass it on right away. So as k goes up, V must fall, and vice versa:

$$k=\frac{1}{V}.$$

Macroeconomists turn the Equation of Exchange into a forecasting tool by making different assumptions about the stability of V. If V is constant for extended periods of time, then the Equation of Exchange indicates that positive changes in the money supply must lead to positive changes in nominal GDP. Once full employment is reached, more money must then be purely inflationary. If V is not constant, however, monetary policy is filled with far more uncertainty. Changes in the quantity of money can short-circuited through fluctuations in V.

Concluding Remarks

This chapter defined macro terms and concepts that you'll encounter on the evening news or in business articles on the U.S. economy. In the process, we looked at the history of money— something to dazzle your intellectual friends—and a description of national product accounts— something to put them asleep.

The technical understanding of the monetary and product dynamics, both piece-by-piece and through the conceptual framework of Say's Law of Markets and the Equation of Exchange, paves the way for the theoretical discussions about the best approach for increasing the wealth of a nation. You know how to keep score, what key variables to look for, and why significant disagreements can arise among experts in the field. You're close. But there's one final hurdle to leap.

*If you're under thirty and not a liberal, you
don't have a heart; and if you're over thirty
and not a conservative, you don't have a mind.*
—*Winston Churchill*

CHAPTER SIX

IT'S A MACROECONOMIC JUNGLE OUT THERE!

If microeconomics is a carefully constructed jigsaw puzzle, then macroeconomic theory is a jungle thicket. It's one thing to assume rational individuals and efficient markets. It's quite another to leap to the level of the entire economy. Is long-run sustained growth possible? And if so just how is it best achieved? Are markets highly efficient and/or fair? What role must the government play? How often do prisonners' dilemmas, tragedies of the common, and moral hazards arise?

We know that the contemporary environment exerts a strong influence on economic thought. The school of thought that you find most insightful or appealing depends upon your personal outlook. Nine such opinion issues are addressed, and economic liberals are differentiated from economic conservatives.

Ten major schools of economic thought are then explored from left to right. The issues that serve to distinguish the schools from each other are:
- attitudes about price adjustments in individual markets,
- views towards monetary policy and the overall price level,
- conclusions about full-employment equilibrium and Say's Law, and
- demands for government redistribution of market-earned income.

Major contributors are given for each school of thought. Each economist listed may not agree exactly with the summary points for the particular school. My intent is to provide the "generally accepted" perspective. Three appendices list the recipients of the Nobel Prize in economics since its inception in 1969 (only those alive may be nominated for the award), the recipients of the John Bates Clark Award winners since 1947 (presented by the American Economic Association every other year to the top economist under forty years of age), and the Chairs of the U.S. Council of Economic Advisors since its inception in 1946. Best of luck keeping all the characters straight in the soap opera of modern economics.

Personal Outlook

As my banking friends are quick to point out, "Everyone carries baggage." Each of us is unique in terms of experiences, how we lived our lives up to now, and physical traits that define us. Gender, skin color, height, and attractiveness play significant roles for all in the alternatives confronted and the paths chosen in life. Our parents, our place of birth, and our siblings are binding constraints in our everyday lives.

But let's go beyond personal appearance and family constraints to consider nine individual factors that shape our economic outlook.

- **The desire for stability and security.** Do you like things to remain basically the same and see the world typically in states of equilibrium, as so many in the western world do? Or do you like significant change, with the world characterized by markets in disequilibrium or even chaos? If you do desire overall stability, what is the best way to sustain it? In particular, can individuals live "freely" without widespread government restrictions and still have a "safe" society?
- **The intelligence of others.** Do you think that the large majority of people in society are essentially intelligent individuals, quite capable of understanding fairly complex issues, and who react consistently in a rational manner? Or do you think that, by and large, the majority of people are often misguided fools, incapable of keeping up on complex issues? And even if you think that the majority of people are individually intelligent, do you think the group

also behaves rationally? Can the various conflicts between the group and the individual be systematically averted so that harmful paradoxes and dilemmas can be avoided?

- **Relevant time horizon.** Are you focused on the immediate present? Or do you take a longer-run viewpoint? In the grasshopper-ant fable where ants prepare for winter while grasshoppers dance, with whom do you most associate?
- **Moral and ethical values.** Similarly, how much do you believe life is to be lived according to moral and religious principles? Do you see great conflict between secular and spiritual thinking, or is harmony possible between the two? How do your moral and spiritual values shape your time horizon, degrees of envy, and sense of optimism or pessimism.
- **Envy for others' success.** Do you believe that the vast majority of people who have success or wealth deserve it because they have earned it through hard work or bright ideas? Or do you envy and resent people at the top because they are there for "unfair" reasons such as cheating, insider trading, collusion, or blind luck?
- **Degree of self-confidence.** Do you believe that you exercise significant control over your life, that you have achieved a great deal because of special talents you have, and that essentially you like where and who you are now? Or do you constantly feel that life is overwhelming, that you wish that you could do many things over, and that you have been short-changed in talents relative to those around you?
- **Desire for differentiation and diversity in life.** Do you love outlandish ideas, want to be around people with divergent viewpoints, and don't care if people have spiked hair or heavily-pierced body parts? Or do you prefer homogeneity in society, decrying social misfits and condemning current attitudes because they spell doom for the U.S. and the rest of the world? Do you yearn for the "good old days"? Is there too much or too little diversity in the world?

- ***Degree of optimism relative to pessimism.*** One of Winston Churchill's famous quotes is, "A pessimist sees the difficulty in every opportunity; an optimist sees the opportunity in every difficulty." Is the world around you filled with many wonderful features and the right circumstances? Do you see the benefits over the costs? And do you trust the invisible hand?
- ***First economics course.*** Never fail to recognize that your first economics teacher has had a marked impact on your view of "truth" in economies. Was this person an impassioned free-trade capitalist who defended free markets? Or was it someone who was a harsh critic of *laissez-faire* capitalism and who felt that substantial government intervention was needed? Did you learn economics from someone who clearly loved the subject matter and lived it practically for years? Or did you learn economics from someone who didn't seem to care, or who couldn't get ideas across, or who despised most other economists? (Please be aware of the brainwashing that may have occurred in the last case.)

The Left and Right: Economic Liberals Versus Economic Conservatives

Webster's New World Dictionary definition of *liberal* ranges from "giving freely, generous" to "being tolerate of views differing from one's own broad-minded" to "favoring political reforms tending toward democracy with personal freedom for the individual" to "disregarding accepted rules and standards".

Economic liberals, as the term is used today, consider themselves extremely generous and well-intentioned. They constantly fret about the plight of the masses. The fruits of production must be spread more fairly. Long-term laws, rules, and regulatory standards must be replaced (as they were in the New Deal) if the old ways are preventing the advancement of the working class. Considerable tolerance of unconventional lifestyles, rather than narrow-mindedness, is mandatory to reduce conflict.

118

At the same time, the liberal view holds that really smart people at the top must be observed constantly to prevent collusion and trickery. Free markets do not provide enough public goods like natural wetlands and old-wood forests. Greed is too pervasive to be left to the invisible hand. The answer is to have fiscal and monetary policy manipulated by the federal government to achieve full-employment and eliminate surplus supplies of labor for greater equity. Today, economic liberals lie "on the left".

Webster's New World Dicionary definition of *conservative* ranges from "conserving or tending to conserve" to "tending to preserve established traditions or institutions and to resist or oppose any changes in these" to "moderate, cautious, and safe". *Economic conservatives* see themselves as preservers of *laissez-faire* capitalism. They too are well-intentioned, only now the emphasis is on individual responsibility, personal saving, capital formation, and individual innovation as the keys to national prosperity. To change well-established market outcomes and define new "moral" standards because certain groups scream discrimination penalizes the wrong people too often. Scarcity means somebody will always be complaining.

If the established order is to be upset, it must be done primarily through the forces of creative destruction and improvements in efficiency, not through arbitrary redistribution or outright confiscation of wealth and property. Only then is it the "right thing to do". Economic conservatives are distrustful of antitrust policy, high taxes, and government intrusion into personal lives. To quote Ronald Reagan, "The nine most dangerous words in the English language are, 'I'm from the government and I'm here to help.'"

Naturally, both the economic left and right argue that theirs is the most correct, most humane, and most promising perspective on modern life. Ultimately, both sides want the same objective: to create economic wealth and to spread it as widely as possible on this earth. Both sides want more utils or "jolts of joy" that signal happiness. The fundamental debate is how much to let individualistic the forces of the marketplace to operate "freely" in order to producee the wealth of nations.

Ten Macroeconomic Schools of Thought
Starting with Adam Smith

The four issues that differentiate the schools of macroeconomic thought start with attitudes on value determination and price adjustments. Just how prevalent are purely competitive markets in the real world? Next, what is the role of money and credit in the economy. In particular, just how much worry should be directed towards inflation? Third comes the perceived stability of capitalism at full employment through Say's Law. In particular, governments have to deficit spend to maintain full employment? The fourth issue is the perceived need for the redistribution of income by the government in the name of equity. Specifically, must the government continually protect the poor and downtrodden?

Table 6.1 summarizes the following discussions of the schools of thought. Let's begin with Adam Smith right in the middle of things, then we'll swing sharply to the left.

Adam Smith and the Classical School

Adam Smith and his Classical School disciples are the basic demarcation between the left and right in Table 6.1, falling just on the conservative side of the spectrum. While Smith admired the wonderful properties of free trade and *laissez-faire* markets, his thinking was somewhat clouded by a labor theory of value that led him to defend the agricultural sector. Also, he did not embrace free trade as Commissioner of Customs and Salt Duties in Edinburgh. Overall, he accepted much more government market intervention in day-to-day life than most *laissez-faire* economists tolerate today.

Monetarily, we know that Smith argued for a real-bills doctrine. He believed that the banking industry needed a central bank in order to maintain security. The central bank facilitates the full gold standard, but it does not play an activist role in the determination of the overall quantity of money in existence. This is left to the discovery of

Economics: An Examination of Scarcity

Table 6.1

TEN MACROECONOMIC SCHOOLS

LEFT						RIGHT			
SOCIALIST/LIBERAL						**CONSERVATIVE/LIBERTARIAN**			

LEFT — SOCIALIST/LIBERAL
- Groupness and necessary coercion
- Really smart people must be watched constantly for fear of collusion
- Many public goods are necessary for present and future generations
- Money/credit conditions are manipulated by government to maintain full employment

RIGHT — CONSERVATIVE/LIBERTARIAN
- Individualism and voluntary exchange
- Really smart, honest people reap "just" rewards
- Private property must be defended by fair laws and courts
- "Sound" money to keep inflation low

The Far Left	Founding British Keynesians	Early American Keynesians	Post-Eclectic Keynesians	Classical School	Marshallian Macroeconomics	The Chicago School and Monetarism	Rational Expectations	Supply Siders	The Far Right: Austrian Libertarians
T. Malthus K. Marx F. Engels O. Lange P. Sweezy P. Ehrlich	J. M. Keynes J. Robinson R. Harrod J. Hicks	A. Hansen P. Samuelson J. Galbraith W. Leontief L. Klein W. Heller J. Tobin F. Modigliani R. Solow E. Domar	H. Stein J. Stiglitz L. Tyson A. Blinder L. Summers L. Thurow P. Krugman S. Fischer R. Eisner	A. Smith J.B. Say D. Ricardo	A. Marshall C. Pigou I. Fisher	M. Friedman R. Coase G. Becker G. Stigler F. Knight J. Buchanan A. Schwartz K. Brunner A. Meltzer J. Jordan *(Haller)*	R. Lucas T. Sargent N. Wallace R. Barro	R. Mundell A. Laffer J. Wanniski A. Reynolds J. Kemp	C. Menger E. Bohm-Bawerk F. Weiser L. Mises J. Schumpeter F.A. Hayek A. Rand
Labor theory of value	Demand and cost conditions set prices in markets with frictions and imperfections			Labor theory of value	Demand and supply conditions set prices in highly competitive markets				
Banks a tool of the system	Monetary policy to accommodate fiscal policy; gold a relic; gold bullion standard	Quantity of money doesn't matter, peg interest rates	Use monetary policy to help drive down the rate of unemployment; don't fret too much about inflation, fiscal policy and price controls can offset easy monetary policy	Real bills doctrine anchored by gold	Full gold standard	Simple money rule	Perhaps a simple money rule, perhaps a real bills doctrine	Full gold standard with central banks	Full gold standard without central banks
No Say's Law, indeed prolonged unemployment and even labor revolt are possible				Say's Law	Say's Law	Natural rate Hypothesis	Say's Law	Full-employment only with low taxes	Business cycles through creative destruction
The economics of envy and the need for government-directed redistribution			Some redistribution of income to the poor is moral			Yeah for profit-maximizers! and the marginal productivity principle of distribution			

INCOME THEORY — **PRICE THEORY**

Adam Smith - Moral Philosophy ✓

The Inquiry into the Nature & Causes of the Wealth of Nations gold along with bankers' perceptions of "real bills" needed in the marketplace. Money growth moves up and down with the business cycle, with boom times creating too much credit and inflation.

Smith rejected overproduction of commodities economy-wide. He concurred with Say's Law because he felt that most saving is promptly invested or spent. The prevalence of scarcity rules out prolonged surpluses of goods or labor in Smith's view.

Finally, in terms of market freedoms, Smith worried about a possible conspiracy to raise prices when people of the same trade get together. Government intervention was, therefore, necessary to keep collusive firms in check. At the same time, he believed that the poorer members of society must be helped by those successful individuals who have shared moral sentiments and want to live a benevolent life. Extensive government welfare is counterproductive.

Swinging to the Far Left: Malthus, Neo-Malthusians, Marx-Engels, and Neo-Marxians

The general optimism about capitalism found in the *Wealth of Nations* soon came under attack, most notably by Thomas Malthus in *An Essay on the Principle of Population, As It Affects the Future Improvement of Society* (1798). This work was first published anonymously for fear of reprisals. Malthus too accepted the labor theory of value and a gold standard. However, unlike the disciples of the Classical School, Malthus rejected Say's Law of Markets and felt that prolonged oversaving was possible.

Malthus percieved unrestrained sexual activity of the human race, the so-called "passion between the sexes". Population growth will inevitably outstrip economic growth in the long run because societies are characterized by the Iron Law of Wages. Further division and specialization of labor won't be enough to offset the surplus supply of people. Free trade makes the situation worst for the masses by causing more rapid population growth. Wages will eventually settle at subsistence levels—it's cast in iron!

In the famous Corn Law debates in 1815, Malthus argued for government tariffs (price floors) on imported corn and grains. He felt that England could only support so many people above poverty levels. In addition, higher corn prices signal a better standard of living, and so they lead to slower population growth. Ricardo challenged the Malthusian perspective immediately with the notion of comparative advantage in defense of free trade. Even so the Corn Laws were passed in 1815 and not repeated until 1846.

For the following 100 years, Malthusian population theory was pushed aside by mainstream economists due to the obvious marked improvements in living standards in western societies. However, in the later 1960's a revival of neo-Malthusian thought occurred. The biologist Paul Ehrlich of Stanford authored of *The Population Bomb* (1970), decrying a tragedy of the commons taking place globally. He called for the first Earth Day at this time. Similarly, Jay Forrester and Dennis Meadows of MIT plus the Club of Rome developed neo-Malthusian computer models in the early 1970's that predicted dire shortages of major raw materials like oil and natural gas and global catastrophe within fifty years due to overpopulation. The world was beyond its optimum carrying capacity!

Karl Marx, along with his close friend and corroborator Friedrich Engels, took the attacks on capitalism well beyond Malthus and overpopulation. First in the *Communist Manifesto* in 1848, and then in *Das Kapital* in 1867, they railed against labor exploitation, not overpopulation, as the primary reason for the misery of the working class. They considered Malthusian thinking "a vile and infamous doctrine, a repulsive blasphemy against man and nature". Instead, science clearly demonstrated that human progress can outstrip population growth if labor exploitation can be avoided. Darwin's *The Origin of Species* appeared in 1859, and it had a profound effect on Marx and Engels. Just as species evolve, so do economic systems they reasoned. Therefore, there can eventually be one big happy "community" on earth.

Marxian doctrine depends most critically on a labor theory of value (even though Marx really knew that market prices were not determined by labor content). It concludes that *all* countries must evolve in a series of well-defined stages.

Chaos is the initial state of the world, followed by *tribal* societies, in which the means of production and the products of labor are collectively owned and equally shared by the group (this won't occur again until the last stage says Marx). Next are *slave-owning* societies, where the means of production (slave and land) are privately owned by the masters.

Eventually comes *feudalism*, in which kings and queens and their nobles are the principal owners of property. Feudalism imposes order on the chaos of smaller societies, but its inherent contradiction is to be too rigid socially. Status at birth remains fixed over time. So here comes *capitalism*, where the means of production (the factories, the land, the banks) may be widely owned at first.

Indeed the early stages of *laissez-faire* capitalism are just as Smith described. Division and specialization of labor create significant improvements in productivity, and free trade improves living standards for many people. No system is *more efficient* at allocating a society's scarce resources than the *laissez-faire* capitalism.

However, Marx and Engels go on to draw a sharp dichotomy between the capitalists, or *bourgeoisie*, and the workers, or *proletariat*. The proletariat appreciate *laissez-faire* competition and free trade because of the consumption benefits being bestowed. In contrast, the bourgeoisie despise the constant struggle for profits and survival-of-the-fittest mentality. Over time, collusion, lobbying efforts, takeovers, and other such monopolist tendencies.

According to the doctrine, the capitalists are driven by a desire to maintain their rate of return as they invest in new capital plant and equipment. Additional investment, *ceteris paribus*, causes the rate of return to fall due to diminishing returns to capital. This process further intensifies monopoly power as weaker firms fall by the wayside. Ultimately, monopolists dominate the economic landscape rather than *laissez-faire* competition.

The new capital investment is argued to be *labor saving*. This means that machines keep replacing workers, causing more involuntary unemployment. A large "reserve army of unemployed" develops that is comprised of workers who want to work but can't find meaningful jobs. *Surplus labor is everywhere.* Striving to maintain their rates of return, monopoly capitalists readily exploit their workers by taking advantage this surplus to hold down wages. In addition, they use their monopoly power to charge monopoly prices. Goods accumulate on store shelves that the masses can't buy. Workers, the true source of value, are underpaid. Tiny Tim is looking in the window, but the goods are beyond his reach. It just isn't fair!

The monopoly capitalism stage persists until the exploitation becomes so demeaning that the workers throw off their chains, ignite a revolution, and take over the means of production. The stage of *socialism* ensues. The established government is thrown out in one fell swoop since the state has been the device controlled by the *bourgeoisie* to advance its own interest. Democracy in the *bourgeois* state is viewed as a complete sham. The *proletariat* seizes power at this catastrophic, yet opportune moment, and the established government dissolves. The *proletariat* forms its own dictatorship and "crushes all capitalist employers along with their distorted class ideology." This stage of socialism is also the beginning of *communism*.

In the distant future, the time will come when this *proletarian* state and its agencies of oppression will wither away according to Marxian doctrine. A new communal psychology arises in which each person is motivated to contribute to the common effort ("from each according to his abilities") and consume only what is necessary ("to each according to his needs"). This second stage is called *full communism*, a world that needs no government because of the abundance of wealth. It is a world in perfect harmony and peace. How paradoxical that "communism" has come to mean complete, totalitarian, government control. Marx defined it as just the opposite.

Marx and Engels readily accepted a gold standard as necessary for exchange. However, they saw the banking and credit system as much of the problem with capitalism. The development and refinement of the financial industry accelerates the concentration of monopoly power and heightens the influence of the *bourgeoisie*. Banks become tools of the capitalists to exploit the workers. Therefore, the financial system has to be "socialized" in the revolution of the *proletariat*. Credit must be rationed by the state. It must be lent to carefully chosen sectors of the economy at interest rates far below market values (even zero). Redistribution of income from capital to labor becomes one of the highest priorities of the state so that all workers receive their true productive value.

What a story! Greed and exploitation are intertwined with disequilibrium and chaos. Overabundance of wealth is only enjoyed by an extreme minority in advanced capitalism. Willing workers suffer at the expense of machines. An enlightened few must become the saviors of the masses. Social perfection on earth is the ultimate goal. Religion is scorned as the "opiate of the masses."

We all know that Marxian leaders like Lenin, Stalin, and Chairman Mao Zedong have bent these ideas to their own dementia. The clear outcome of Marxian doctrine, when applied in the political arena, has been the mass exploitation and suffering that Marx himself condemned. Perhaps Marx anticipated such turmoil when, on his deathbed, he said, "I am not a Marxist!"

The radical left of today clings to the belief that if the social evils of capitalism are eliminated, the true and wonderful nature of the human race will blossom. Religious thought is irrational. Concentrate instead on the secular world, and use applied science to determine exploitation and the means to manage it.

In the 1940's and 1950's, neo-Marxian economists like Oskar Lange and Paul Sweezy (of kinked demand curve fame) tried to advance Marx-Engels ideology in the U.S. But even with the swing left in the economics profession after World War II, they faced opposition to their harsh anti-Marshallian micro viewpoint. A minor revival of Marxian macro dynamics occurred in the 1960's and early 1970's but since the 1980's, the Marxians, like

Malthusians, have been on the run in the economics profession. The basic belief that there are excess supplies of worker and that the human race is doomed in its present stage because of "evil" emotions and actions sells far better among sociologists, anthropologists, and political scientists.

Keep in mind that even though the far left thinkers say they are driven by the desire to improve life for the masses, their prescriptions inevitably assume that the masses are foolish as a group. Either they overproduce offspring or they let themselves be exploited. So it is up to highly-trained, far-sighted individuals, who must outguess markets, to manage the system and people properly. What's there left to do?

Founding British Keynesians

If a vote had been taken in the 1960's among professional economists as to who is the most influential economic thinker of the 20th century, the runaway victor would have been John Maynard Keynes. And he still might win today. Keynes was born in 1883, the year Marx died. His father was a professor of political economy at Cambridge and his mother served as mayor of Cambridge. Keynes lived a highly productive and rewarding scholarly life as a young man, first at Eton and later at King's College, Cambridge University. He moved to India for several years before becoming a consultant to the British Treasury in 1911.

Keynes first achieved international fame at the end of World War I with his criticism of the Treaty of Versailles in *The Economic Consequences of Peace* (1920). He foresaw that the Treaty would devastate the Germany and lead the German people towards another world conflict. Soon thereafter, in *The Economic Consequences of Mr. Churchill* (1925), he criticized Winston Churchill's plan to return England to a full gold standard at pre-war parity, arguing that it would reduce world-wide liquidity and shrink international trade. Keynes was correct on both accounts. His magnus opus, *The General Theory of Employment, Interest, and Money* (1936), appeared in the midst of the Great Depression. It gained widespread acceptance among mainstream

British intellectual society and generated immediate disciples in the economic profession. Before we take up *The General Theory*, however, we must consider the Marshallian macroeconomic arguments at the end of the 19th century.

Marshallian Macroeconomics

Let's rely upon the Equation of Exchange, MV = PQ, to see what Marshall and his followers had to say about the macro economy. They wrote at the height of the Victorian Age, and all was right in England. It was a time of grand stability. At the micro level, we know that the Marshallians took a partial-equilibrium perspective to demonstrate how *laissez-faire* markets work naturally to eliminate shortages or surpluses through the interaction of demand and supply. Relative prices adjust until market equilibrium is achieved.

Extending this reasoning to the Say's Law debate, Marshallians were well-aware that a complex monetary economy has both financial injections and financial leakages. Too much saving, a leakage, could cause an accumulation of goods on producers' shelves. But the problem was only temporary. Nominal interest rates, which are the prices of loanable funds for firms and of savings for households, would adjust.

Like all prices, interest rates are determined by the two "blades" of demand and of supply. When too much desired savings (a leakage) occurs relative to desired investment (an injection), a decline in interest rates will result. The decline then increases desired investment while reducing desired savings. The surplus in savings is eliminated efficiently by the marketplace. The conclusion is that Say's Law holds even in complex monetary economics as long as interest rates are flexible.

In addition, if workers really want to work, they will accept lower wages when they are unemployed. Likewise, if goods remain on the shelves too long, firms will cut money prices to sell more output. So labor and product markets adjust to full-employment equilibrium even if interest rates do not move much. Say's Law continues to operate as long as wages and prices are flexible.

Capitalism is inherently stable at full employment in the long run because the PRICE MECHANISM functions smoothly (that's why it's called price theory). For the Equation of Exchange, Q will grow at its full-employment potential in the long run, perhaps 4 percent for the U.S.

In terms of monetary policy, the Marshallians favored a full gold standard. They carefully distinguished between the quantity stock of money in circulation and the subsequent creation of credit via related financial instruments. With a gold standard, the quantity of money cannot be produced arbitrarily at the government's will. Instead, a country must define its national currency per ounce of gold and not create any additional money stock unless it has more gold imports or discovers more gold, or the public deposits gold in banks. For the Equation of Exchange, M grows at at a fairly steady rate (2-3% per year on average in the U.S. over the last part of the 19th century).

Marshallians believed that the velocity of money (V) is constant for extended periods. The primary reason households and firms demand money (cash balances) is to conduct transactions. This demand is determined primarily by slow changing institutional factors, such as how often people are paid each month. Consequently, the demand for cash balances (k) is a constant fraction of nominal GDP ($M_D=kPQ$). Here money is a "veil". Money supply growth sets the absolute price level (P), but it has no *real* effects on Q since *relative* price adjustments maintain Say's Law.

Wealth is distributed in the marketplace to individuals according to the "value of their marginal product", defined as the selling price of the product times the marginal product of the worker. This is the *marginal productivity principle of distribution*. It leads to the conclusion that because workers are paid the value of their marginal product in production, those who have the greatest wealth must be the most productive in supplying what society wants most. The market speaks through the laws of demand and supply and, "survival of the fittest".

Chapter 6

Marshallians felt that the government has no right to interfere with the "free" movement across borders of legally-earned income, currency, gold bullion, goods and services or for that matter people themselves. It does not have any right to set highly progressive income taxes in order to take from the rich and give to the poor. The rich themselves should be allowed to decide how to help society. Indeed, they are expected to do so, as exemplified by "robber barons" like Carnegie, Stanford, Duke, and Rockefeller who gave much of their huge wealth back to society in charitable ways.

Marshallian macroeconomics is a scientific update of the *Wealth of Nations*. Demand and supply replace the labor theory of value, and a full gold standard replaces a real-bills doctrine. Yet both Smith and the Marshallians are deeply committed to free markets and free trade. Both see the economic role of the government as a referee rather than as a central planner, and both see the necessity for annually balanced budgets rather than federal deficits. There is continued faith in the invisible hand to channel individual self-interests into the wealth of nations.

In Table 6.1 the Marshallian school is placed slightly to the right of the Classical School because of the stronger belief in both the efficiency and equity of free markets (due to the hindsight of seeing the advances of the industrial revolution) plus th rejection of the real-bills doctrine. Before we leave Marshallian macroeconomics, let's consider two of its theoretical effects that practical implications.

(1) The Pigou Effect

When Marshall retired from his chair of political economy at Cambridge in 1908, the position was filled by C. A. Pigou, one of his distinguished students. Pigou subsequently made significant contributions to microeconomic (his three degrees of price discrimination are but one example).

At the macroeconomic level he formulated the famous *Pigou effect* (or *real wealth effect*). During the Great Depression, Keynesian economists argued that falling nominal wages would not eliminate unemployment. Falling nominal wages would be accompanied by a falling absolute price level of the same amount, so real wages $\left(\frac{W\downarrow}{P\downarrow}\right)$ would remain the same. No additional purchasing power is generated for an economy.

Pigou countered that the falling absolute price level would increase the public's *real cash balances* $\left(\frac{\overline{M2}}{P\downarrow}\right)$ if the nominal money stock remains constant. The higher real balances and positive wealth effect stimulate consumer spending and reduce unemployment. Therefore, capitalistic, free-market economies have an important self-correcting *price* mechanism at the macro level, just as at the micro level, as long as the money supply is constant.

(2) Irving Fisher: A Compensated Dollar and the Fisher Effect

Irving Fisher of Yale University is often considered the brightest American economist of the early 20th century. Fisher was a firm believer in Say's Law. He's been vilified for advising his large investment clients to aggressively buy after the Crash in 1929 because of his staunch belief that capitalism was inherently stable in the long run.

He also favored a gold standard, but one based on a "compensated dollar". The actual weight of gold backing for each dollar would vary to keep the purchasing power of the dollar constant over time relative to a price index of a select number of goods. If the price index rose, more grains of gold would be added to the dollar, and visa versa. Rather than the money supply tied strictly to gold, it would be tied to a market basket of goods to achieve greater price stability through diversification.

Fisher's name is most often linked with his pioneering work on interest rates. Drawing extensively upon the ideas of the Austrian School (notably Böhm-Bawerk), Fisher's *The Rate of Interest* (1907) and *The Theory of Interest* (1930) used modern economic tools (indifference curves and production possibility curves) to demonstrate that real interest rates are determined by two basic factors. The first is the preference of people for present goods rather than future goods. The other is the productivity of capital goods. The equilibrium interest rate for the economy is where the desired demand of loanable funds equals the desired supply of loanable funds, just as we would expect.

Out of this analysis comes one of the most important forecasting equations in macroeconomics. The *Fisher equation* is:

nominal interest rate = a real rate of interest
plus a rate of inflationary
expectations.

The *Fisher effect* concerns inflation. Because creditors can be hurt by inflation, any *expected* rise in the rate of inflation is added to the real interest rate in order to offset the loss of purchasing power due to inflation. The Fisher effect means that rapid increases in the money supply must ultimately create higher nominal interest rates. In the short run, a burst in the money supply may drive down nominal rates. But sooner or later households and firms anticipate more inflation from monetary growth. Nominal interest rates then go up sharply as lenders try to protect themselves from "cheapened" dollars.

A Return to the Founding British Keynesians

Keynes' *The General Theory of Employment, Interest and Money* appeared on the scene in 1936. The arrogance was stunning even for the economics profession. This was to be THE theory – not just A theory – of employment, interest AND money! Indeed, it was to be GENERAL THEORY rather than an introduction or primer. Keynes had become a legendary London speculator/investor, and he possessed extreme confidence in his forecasting abilities (not unreasonable given his insights about the Treaty of Versailles and England's return to the gold standard). Moreover, he was an extremely gifted political essayist and traveled with the fast British intellectual crowd.

The General Theory was intended to save capitalism from the grips of the state central planning mentality that was sweeping across the world in the 1930's. Like Malthus and Marx, Keynes saw oversaving as a distinct possibility. And like Marx, he felt that excessive unemployment was the fundamental economic problem confronting mature, capitalistic economies. Even so, Keynes rejected much of Marxian political theory: "How can I accept a doctrine which sets up as its Bible, above and beyond criticism, an obsolete economics textbook which I know to be not only scientifically erroneous but without interest or application for the modern world?"

Keynes was one of Marshall's brightest students. Yet in contrast to the Marshallian world of freely competitive markets, *The General Theory* argued that monopolies and labor unions dominate mature, capitalistic economies. Prices and wages are not flexible downward when goods accumulate and surplus labor is present. Firms lay off workers before cutting prices, and unions hold nominal wages constant through layoffs or strikes. INCOME rather than PRICE is the prime adjustment variable (that's why it's called income theory). In the end, capitalism can settle down for long periods of time at less than the full employment level of GDP.

Keynes' British disciples, notably Joan Robinson and Roy Harrod at Cambridge University, provided mathematical models showing how labor wages are distorted through exploitation, that product prices are distorted by imperfect competition, and that the long-run potential growth path will be a knife's edge for an economy. Government intervention is needed throughout the economy to offset the friction and imperfects in real world markets.

According to Keynes, business cycles are the result of volatile investment spending due to the "animal spirits" of investors. They move in herds or like schools of fish darting about. A capitalist economy may boom for periods as investors create profits through new ideas. Desired leakages and injections may actually be equal at the aggregate level of full employment. But eventually excesses must develop. Too much investment creates over-capacity in industry. Households increase savings in anticipation of a downturn. Unwanted inventories accumulate. Investors start to run scared and cut back on further investment. Workers are laid off and involuntary unemployment rises. The falling incomes may mean households may actually end up saving less than they planned due to the paradox of thrift.

Declining interest rates do not directly link saving and investment plans, according to *The General Theory*, because interest rates are a monetary rather than a real saving-investment phenomenon. Interest rates are determined by the intersection of the demand for cash balances and the supply of cash balances, not by the demand and supply of loanable funds as the Marshallians believed. Instead of the simple transactions approach to the demand for money of the Marshallians, *The General Theory* stresses that money demand arises due to both transactions needs *and* liquidity/uncertainty needs.

For individual households, interest rates are a necessary payment that must be received to part with liquidity. Given the choice between either holding cash or investing in bonds, falling interest rates cause households to hold more cash rather than to invest in risky bonds. As bond prices go up as interest rates go down, there is some "low" nominal rate where households will only want to hold cash rather than take big risks on high-priced bonds. This is the so-called Keynesian *liquidity trap*.

For firms, interest rates are the cost of borrowing. Investment decisions are undertaken if Keynes' *marginal efficiency of capital* (the internal rate of return of a project) is greater than the prevailing nominal market interest rate. At the margin, falling market interest rates cause additional investment projects to be undertaken, *ceteris paribus*. At the same time, falling market rates do not stimulate investment spending if expectations of future profits are plunging as well.

All things considered, monetary policy can only drive down interest rates only so low to try to eliminate recession. It is like "pushing the economy with a string". Liquidity traps, dampened animal spirits, saving fears, and the hoarding of currency/credit short-circuit the financial system. Active fiscal policy – government taxation and spending – is the answer, specifically *functional finance* in which government finances serve the function of "balancing the economy" rather than "balancing the federal budget annually."

Supply does not create its own demand in the Keynesian world. Instead, for the economy as a whole, DEMAND CREATES ITS OWN SUPPLY. As long as the "proper" level of total spending is maintained, goods won't accumulate on the shelves and cyclical unemployment will be minimal. To offset the downward shift of total spending in a recession, the federal government has various options. It can cut taxes. Or it can enlarge welfare payments. Or it can undertake various public work projects like roads and dams. Or it can try to stimulate exports, through devaluation of the currency.

Keynes considered gold "a barbarous relic". He believed that a pure gold standard restricts the economy unfairly. Instead, management of the money supply and credit by the government is necessary to encourage full employment and peak production. The harsh free-market nature of a full gold standard must be replaced by a gold bullion standard. Even government external credit controls may be necessary. Because interest rates have a marginal impact on investment spending, the primary domestic role of central banks is to continually "peg" nominal interest rates up or down to affect total investment spending.

In terms of the Equation of Exchange, the founding British Keynesians see both Q and V as highly volatile. Consequently, any changes in M on nominal GDP are unpredictable. The government has to influence Q directly through aggregate spending. In the process, wage and price controls, industrial policy, increased government spending, and highly-expansionary monetary policy are all fair game. Politically, depressions must be avoided at all costs. Firms and households must come to expect the government to spend, spend, spend rather than sit on the sidelines when unemployment is high. Keep M and V rising, impose restrictions on P, and Q will keep growing.

The founding British Keynesians, like Robin Hood, defended the idea of taking of money from the rich and giving it to the poor. The rich save a larger proportion of their income than the poor.

Thus, by taxing the rich progressively to provide welfare payments to the poor, the flow of total spending actually increases, both directly and through subsequent *multiplier effects*.

Keynes, as a consultant to the British Treasury office, helped formulate the Bretton Woods Agreement in 1944. The Marshall Plan immediately after WWII drew upon his ideas in *The Economic Consequences of Peace*. The Employment Act of 1946 stating that the U.S. government would actively try to maintain full employment, was clearly in line with his thinking. The "Keynesian revolution" had begun. Then Keynes died in 1946.

Early American Keynesians

The Keynesian invasion beachhead in the U.S. was Cambridge, Massachusetts. In the later 1930's John Kenneth Galbraith at Harvard avidly read *The General Theory* and taught John Kennedy basic economics, while Alvin Hansen started influencing a generation of outstanding graduate students led by Paul Samuelson. During World War II, Galbraith was in charge of U.S. price controls, a testimony to his political savvy. After the war, Hansen, along with Nobel laureate John Hicks, popularized the famous IS-LM model of the economy. With interest rates on the vertical axis and real GDP on the horizontal axis, the real side of the economy (the IS or "investment-saving" side) is combined with the financial side of economy (the LM or "liquidity-money" side) in order to demonstrate the need for Keynesian fiscal policy to maintain full employment.

Paul Samuelson received his Ph.D. from Harvard in 1941 and ultimately established the MIT economics department. His best-selling *Economics* textbook, first published in 1948, introduced the world to the Keynesian "cross diagrams", those graphs with the 45-degree straight line serving as the aggregate supply curve and the C+I+G+(X-M) aggregate demand curve. Samuelson's first Ph.D. graduate in economics from MIT, Lawrence Klein, developed the well-known Wharton econometric model of the U.S. economy in the early 1950's.

Galbraith's *Affluent Society* appeared in 1958, railing against the capitalistic attitude that produced tail fins for cars rather than better schools for children. Franco Modigliani of MIT was formulating an extensive lifecycle theory of consumption and saving, while James Tobin of Yale developed the microeconomic foundations of modern financial theory. In the process, the early American Keynesians rejected the simple quantity theory of money as proposed by Marshallians. The early American Keynesians concluded that money is just another asset that households hold in their portfolio. What matters is *not* the total quantity of money in circulation. Instead, what matters is the overall availability of credit and the pegging of interest rates.

The American Keynesians felt the need to build their macroeconomic arguments on Marshallian micro foundations. In particular, they wanted to show that aggregate behavior is consistent with individual maximization. This led to a *neoclassical synthesis* of the mid-1950's. Tobin demonstrated that the upward sloping LM curve is consistent with individual maximization of financial portfolios, and Modigliani used the idea that individual households maximize their consumption over a lifetime as the basis for his theory of spending and saving.

Then along comes the *Phillips curve*. Named after its originator A. W. Phillips (1958), the first Phillips curve compared percentage changes in money wages to unemployment rates in the U.K. from 1861 to 1957. It found an inverse relationship, and one that looked quite stable. Subsequently, inflation rates were substituted for money wage rates by American Keynesians, and through the 1960's they felt that their Phillips curve was one of the most stable of all macro relationships: rising inflation means lower unemployment, and vice versa. Accordingly, the U.S. economy could be "fine-tuned" to an acceptable combination of unemployment and inflation. Mathematical growth theory models by Robert Solow and Evsey Domar showed the precise paths to follow to achieve optimal growth over time.

The American Keynesian theoretical explanation for the stable Phillips curve lies in labor markets. Labor markets are disequilibrium. Excess demand for certain labor coexists with overall unemployment and excess supply. Imperfections and frictions in the labor market— lack of information, heterogeneity of workers, and mismatch of jobs—mean that job vacancies are not filled immediately even with an overall excess supply of labor. The "persistent" excess demand in certain labor markets is explained by stickiness or rigidity in nominal wages that prevent these markets from clearing. As labor markets in general tightened and the unemployment rate falls, inflation must occur. Goods prices are driven up by higher nominal wages. There is *cost-push* inflation and an apparently stable Phillips curve.

In 1961, Walter Heller, President Kennedy's Chair of the CEA, led the charge for income tax cuts. The unemployment rate was above 4 percent, the accepted definition of full-employment by the American Keynesians, and they saw fine-tuning possibilities. The income tax cuts of 1964 were a resounding success. The Keynesians revolution achieved its greatest single moment.

The huge influence of the Keynesian revolution from 1965 to 1969 coincided with my undergraduate years at the University of Missouri in Columbia. It was a time of marvelous hope among economists. Both economic fine-tuning and the achievement of a Great Society using social scientific principles seemed possible.

Unfortunately, U.S. budget deficits exploded in 1967 and 1968 as President Johnson tried to finance both the Viet Nam War and his Great Society. The Fed monetized the deficits by purchasing large amounts of U.S. government securities from the U.S. Treasury. Combined with the U.S. dollars already in existence throughout the world, there was not enough gold backing existed for all the federal reserve notes in circulation. Countries demanded payment.

The result was the collapse of the Bretton Woods agreements. The Fed, with President Nixon's blessing, sharply cut the growth of the money supply in 1969 in order to fight inflation.

At the same time, Friedman and others were dismissing the notion of a stable Phillips curve. If inflationary expectations rises, the Phillips curve shifts outward rather than remains stable. Thus the unemployment rate and inflation rate rise simultaneously and "fine-tuning" looks like a joke.

The wage and price controls adopted in turned out to be a disastrous attempt to fine tune. As money flooded into the economy prior to the 1972 election, the Nixon administration at first looks like an economic wonder. Then in 1974 everything comes apart. Inflation hits double digits, and growth turns negative. Friedman's monetarism emerged as a powerful counter-force to Keynesian thought, soon followed by the development of the rational expectations school and the supply-side perspective. By the 1970's, the economics profession was clearly swinging back to the right, especially outside the Boston- D.C corridor.

Post-Eclectic Keynesians

Even with this swing to the right, the presence of a significant number of older American Keynesians, many of them Nobel prize winners, still writing and educating large numbers of bright graduate students, meant that Keynesian economies did not suddenly vanish at the end of the 1970's. Instead, *post-eclectic Keynesians* have emerged.

Influenced by Friedman's work, this group concedes that money does matter significantly for the wealth of nations. Still, activist fiscal policy is necessary to maintain full employment. Basic Keynesians prescriptions work in many cases. The federal government must remain involved in the plight of the poor. Expenditures for the necessary welfare programs must come through tax increases, otherwise the deficits will explode. "Managed" international trade, influenced by selected government objectives like human rights, must take precedence over "free" trade. Domestic credit controls may be necessary to stop domestic money from fleeing across borders. Nations must be prepared to devalue their currencies to eliminate "persistent" trade deficits. Extensive antitrust policy must be used to prevent markets from getting out-of-hand since people like Bill Gates are evil. Central planning from Washington, D.C., exercised with "intelligent" clout and power, is preferable to a free-market economy.

A significant number of the post-eclectic Keynesians have earned their Ph.D.'s from MIT (what a surprise!). Included here are: Joseph Stiglitz who recently served as Chair of the CEA and then chief economist at the World Bank; Laura Tyson who was President Clinton's first Chair of the CEA and is now Dean of the Berkeley Haas School of Business; Lawrence Summers, an undergraduate student at MIT, who is currently Secretary of the U.S. Treasury; Stanley Fischer who is presently Deputy Director of the IMF; Martin Baily who is currently Chair of the CEA; Alan Blinder, who was a vice-chair of the Federal Reserve Board in 1994-96 before returning to the Princeton faculty; and Paul Krugman, professor at Princeton. Lester Thurow, educated at Harvard, and a former dean of the MIT School of Management, is another well-known post-eclectic Keynesian. Lastly, let's not forget Robert Eisner of Northwestern, not MIT educated, but until his death in 1998 one of the most outspoken Keynesian commentators on the editorial page of the *Wall Street Journal* and elsewhere.

The Chicago School and Monetarism

Swinging back to the right, even over Smith and Marshall, the Chicago School of economics has had a proud history of free-market thinking and the application of rational economic thought to a variety of problems. We have already encountered Ronald Coase's famous theorem on externalities and Gary Becker's microeconomics of household fertility, both of whom have been professors at the University of Chicago since the 1970's. Frank Knight exerted a huge influence as a faculty member from 1928 until is death in 1972. F.A. Hayek served as professor of social and moral sciences at the University of Chicago from 1950 to 1962. Nobel laureate George Stigler spent over thirty years at Chicago examining industrial structures and the impact of public regulation in a capitalistic economy.

However, when it comes to public recognition, the Chicago School is most identified today with Milton Friedman, in particular his views on money and personal freedom. Friedman became a professor at Chicago in 1946, the same year that he received his Ph.D. from Columbia University. In the early 1950's he stood against the rising tide of liberal Keynesian thought, defending the model of perfect competition for its useful conclusions and arguing that household consumption is a function of *permanent* income rather than *current* disposable income like Keynesians believed. He also called for the elimination of the Food and Drug Administration for being anti-consumer, a voucher system for education, a simple flat income tax, an "all-volunteer" army, and the legalization of drugs because prohibition just does not work. While Friedman is a self-described libertarian, more often he is referred to as a *monetarist* by the economics profession.

At the macro level, perhaps his greatest claim to fame is the resurrection of the quantity theory of money after trashing it look from the early British and American Keynesians. Along with Anna Schwartz, notably in *A Monetary History of the United States: 1867-1960* which appeared in 1963, Friedman concluded that INFLATION IS ALWAYS AND EVERYWHERE A MONETARY PHENOMENON. Too much money in circulation relative to output growth is the only cause for inflation, not imperfections in labor markets and other cost-push factors. Markets are basically quite efficient. Besides Friedman and Schwartz, other important monetarists include Karl Brunner of the University of Rochester, Alan Meltzer of Carnegie-Mellon, and Jerry Jordon the current president of the Cleveland Federal Reserve. They have tremendous faith in free markets and free trade.

Monetarists believe that the economy is characterized by widespread demand-and-supply competition and that extensive government regulations are unnecessary. Building particularly on the work of Irving Fisher, Friedman and Schwartz originally argued that the demand or velocity of money can be relatively stable for extended periods. Velocity has a secular upward trend

nd technological advances speed up financial
e. In addition, velocity is affected by nominal
opportunity cast of holding cash) and infla-
ons (the opportunity cost of real purchasing
power lost). If nominal interest rates and inflationary expectations are rising sharply, so will the velocity of money. On the
other hand, if they are "low", the velocity of money will stabilize
around its trend line. Using the Equation of Exchange, because V
is stable, growth in M has a direct and predictable effect on PQ.

Friedman has long-argued that individuals have *adaptive
expectations*. In other words, you can trick all of the people
some of the time, some of the people all of the time, but not all
of the people all of the time. They eventually adapt.

He has also argued that the U.S. economy is not inherently
stable at some predefined level of full employment. Instead, the
economy has a *natural rate of unemployment*, defined as the
"level of unemployment, which has the property that it is consistent with equilibrium in the structure of real wage rates". At the
natural rate of employment, real wages tend on average to rise at
a "normal" secular rate. This means that the natural rate of unemployment, coupled with rising real wages, can be indefinitely
maintained as long as capital formation, technological improvements, and other macro forces remain on their long-run trends.

The natural rate of unemployment is not easy to estimate
because it depends upon the particular circumstances of time
and place. Regardless, according to Friedman an accurate estimate is not needed to conduct a proper monetary policy. Above
all, the monetary authority (central bank) must *not* adopt an
arbitrary target of unemployment, say three percent, then be
tight when unemployment is less than the target, be easy when
unemployment is higher than the target, and in this way try to
peg unemployment at three percent. The unemployment rate is
determined "naturally" by the forces of the economy.

The key variable for the monetary authorities to control is
the quantity of money, not the unemployment rate. In particu-

lar, Friedman wants M_2 to grow forever at a constant rate. This rate is the one that is considered the long-run potential growth rate in output. The new money in circulation will then soak up the new real GDP produced in the economy, causing the absolute price index to stabilize over time near zero inflation. Constant growth in M_2 is known as Friedman's *Simple Money Rule*. In terms of the Equation of Exchange,

$$\overset{\uparrow\sim\quad\sim\uparrow}{MV=PQ.}$$

The Simple Money Rule is, paradoxically, anything but simple. It is based upon very careful arguments about competitive markets, personal freedom, and private property as the best means to deal with scarcity and to encourage innovation. It accepts that households and firms can be tricked in the short run, but not in the long run. Therefore, why try to trick the public at all about the growth in the money stock? Discretionary Fed policy often leads to inflation, which is a destabilizing force in the economy.

The reason for the focus on M_2 can be seen in Figure 6.1, which compares 10-year moving averages of M_2, the GNP deflator, and nominal GNP since the 1870's. The long-run association between M_2 and the GNP deflator is apparent. Every major acceleration in M_2 growth has been associated with inflation, and every major deceleration in M_2 growth has been associated with a deceleration in inflation. Inflation does indeed appear to be "always and everywhere a monetary phenomenon" in the U.S.

Friedman suggests that attempts to "fine tune" to smooth out business cycles are likely to make economic conditions worse rather than better. By the time monetary authorities gather the necessary information, process it, and then decide on the appropriate course of action, the real economy has moved on. It can be in an expansionary phase when authorities still believe it is contracting. Consequently, easy monetary policy comes at the wrong time and intensifies the upswing in the business cycle. The same is true of fiscal policy.

In rejecting the inherent stability of capitalism at full-employment, Friedman is highly critical of the Austrian business cycle theorists' response to the Great Depression. In a recent interview in Barron's, he noted that Hayek, while at the London School of Economics in the 1930's with free-market scholar Lionel Robbins, said you just have to let the bottom drop out of the world, you just have to let it cure itself. Encouraging this kind of do-nothing policy both in Britain and the U.S. is wrong according to Friedman.

Figure 6.1

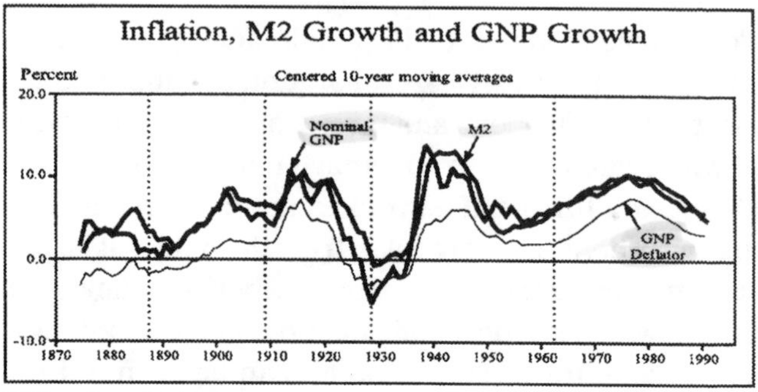

Source: William Dewald, "Inflation: Always a Monetary Phenomenon!", *Monetary Trends*, Federal Reserve Bank of St. Louis, October 1997.

To prevent destructive tampering by elected or appointed government officials, Friedman wants the Simple Money Rule to become a constitutional amendment. He also wants a constitutional amendment for a federally balanced budget to prevent the particularly onerous and persistent increases in the level of government spending. In terms of income redistribution, Friedman favors "negative" income tax for those in the lowest (poorest) income levels, and once the poverty threshold of income is passed, a simple flat tax is then applied to all income levels.

Friedman has been at the Hoover Institute at Stanford University since his retirement from the University of Chicago in 1982. If Marshall is updated Smith, then Friedman is updated Marshall. Exalted by all of these economic thinkers is the freedom to choose, the freedom to trade, and the freedom to enjoy the rewards generated by self-interests *while recognizing the individual consequences.* According to Friedman:

I have always said the essence of a free-market system, which tends to be called a profit-and-lost system, is that the loss component is more important than the profit component. You need the discipline of the loss in order to keep the system going.

The Rational Expectations School

What if households and firms have *rational expectations* rather than Friedman's adaptive expectations? This makes it is impossible to trick people systematically even in the short run. Individuals use all kinds of information at hand rather than relying on animal spirits, feelings, or hunches to make decisions. Their expected economic forecasts, on average, are correct, especially if the government doesn't do something unanticipated with the money supply or fiscal policy. Free markets are incredibly efficient if households and firms know the rules the government is using.

The idea of rational expectations can be traced to work of John Muth from Indiana University in 1961. However, it was Nobel laureate Robert Lucas, then of Carnegie-Mellon and now of the University of Chicago, who advanced the views considerably in the 1970's. Other notable contributors include Tom Sargent of the Hoover Institute and Stanford, Neil Wallace of Penn State University, and Robert Barro of Harvard.

Rational expectations economists they believe that the business cycle is something to be explained rather than to be controlled. The government must be consistent in its policy actions to help reduce the swings in business cycles. For this reason, a Simple Money Rule can make a great deal of economic sense for the U.S. At the same time, Sargent and Wallace (1982) have suggested that a real-bills doctrine or a gold standard may be better alternatives if they can further reduce uncertainty in the economy.

In the absence of unanticipated shocks in monetary or fiscal policy by the government, the U.S. economy adjusts *quickly* back to the natural rate of unemployment when upset by aggregate supply or demand forces. A form of Say's Law prevails: individuals are always maximizing given their constraints, so the economy is normally at or near the best it can do given the circumsances. That is why rational expectations are sometimes referred to as the "new classical economics." They are in the tradition of Smith, Say, and Ricardo. The fundamental difference between rational expectations and the monetarists lies with the perceived speed of adjustment of the economy when shocked. For this reason, the rational expectations crowd is placed slightly to the right of the Chicago School and Monetarism in the layout of macro schools. They have abiding faith in market rationality and efficiency.

The Supply-Sider Perspective

Another group of economists who were highly critical of Keynesian economics in the 1970's were the supply-siders. They drew upon the work of gold standard defenders like recent Nobel laureate Robert Mundell of Columbia University, calling out to restore of monetary santity to the world. In addition, they pushed for large cuts in income taxes and capital gains taxes to reach the full-employment potential of the U.S. economy and to eliminate persistent budget deficits.

The cornerstone of supply-side economics is the Laffer Curve, depicted in Figure 6.2. According to economic lore, this curve was drawn by Arthur Laffer, then of the University of Southern California and now a private consultant, on the back of a cocktail napkin at a Washington D.C. restaurant. Present was Jude Wanniski, a reporter for the *Wall Street Journal*, who subsequently popularized the Laffer Curve through a series of articles.

The Laffer Curve indicates that total tax revenues will initially go up as income tax rates go up, just as Keynesian economics would argue. However, at some rate (say 50 percent) total tax revenues will begin to decline as the tax rates keep increasing. This occurs for two reasons. First, people do not work as hard. Why do overtime work, even at double your normal wages, if the government is going to take away half or more of the additional income? Second, more economic activity is driven into the "underground economy" and away from the tax collectors. Instead of generating an increase in federal tax revenues, high marginal tax rates cause constant federal revenue shortfalls and deficits indefinitely into the future.

Figure 6.2: A Hypothetical Laffer Curve

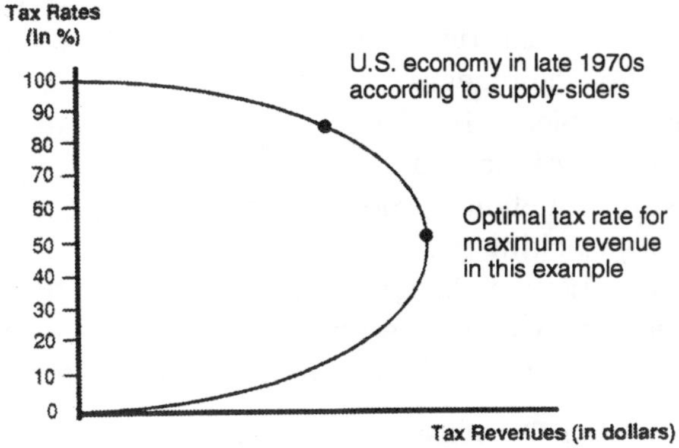

**Tax Rates
(in %)**

U.S. economy in late 1970s
according to supply-siders

Optimal tax rate for
maximum revenue
in this example

Tax Revenues (in dollars)

The Laffer Curve became the basis for the Reagan income tax cuts of 1982-84. It has changed the way the economics profession envisions appropriate fiscal policy in mature capitalist economies. In the past, far too much emphasis was placed on aggregate demand at the expense of aggregate supply in tax and spending models when predicting tax changes on the economy. Today, Laffer runs his own consulting firm and Wanniski is President of Polyconomics in Morristown, N.J. Other notable supply-siders include Alan Reynolds of the Hudson Institute and 1996 Republican vice-presidential candidate Jack Kemp.

Regarding a gold standard, the supply-siders want to have the central bank set the price of gold. For example, Wanniski for the U.S. recently suggested $350 an ounce. Subsequent deviations from this price would then indicate too little or too much liquidity in the system. If the market price of gold rises above $350 an ounce, there is a surplus of liquidity, so the Fed withdraws money from the banking system through open-market sales of government securities. If the market price falls below $350 an ounce, the Fed buys government securities to increase liquidity in the banking system. Once the money stock is anchored in this fashion, Wanniski believes that, "The U.S. dollar would provide a reliable guide to all other national currencies. The global financial maelstroms of the last 30 years would give way to a new century of calm."

In terms of income redistribution, the supply siders are openly hostile to antitrust laws. They strongly oppose the redistribution of entrepreneurs' earned income via the government to welfare recipients. Bill Gates is not evil—he is to be hailed. So are the other innovators and risk-takers who have helped generate the 20 million new jobs since 1993. Envy is a very poor reason for attacking success in the marketplace. The "hard work" ethic must remain alive and well in the U.S by removing the burden of excessive government. Simple flat taxes, very low capital gains taxes, and "never taxing a tax" are the answers.

The Far Right: The Austrian School

By consensus, the *Austrian school* is the most conservative of the major schools of macro thought. It started in the 1870's with Carl Menger's "utils" and relying upon marginal utility for value determination, soon followed by Eugene Böhm-Bawerk's defense of interest rates and payments to capital and Fredrick Wieser's further refinements of "opportunity cost" and "marginal utility". In other words, the Austrian school has been a powerful voice for free markets and personal choice from its onset, and the great Austrian Troika of Menger, Böhm-Bawerk, and Wieser were "classic liberals" in the 19th century sense.

Among the great 20th century Austrians, Ludwig Mises entered the University of Vienna, at the turn of the century, shortly before Joseph Schumpeter, and the two jointly studied under Böhm-Bawerk. Mises became a professor of economics at Vienna in 1913. During the 1920's he rejected the possibility of "rational" resource allocation in socialism because this system cannot solve the economic problem of the pricing of scarce means of production. Most critically, the pricing function of the market cannot be divorced from private ownership of resources and the profit motive. If the prospect of profit vanishes, the market mechanism loses its power to improve general living standards. Because private property is necessary and must be protected, fair courts and sound money are absolutely essential for the invisible hand to prosper.

Joseph Schumpeter, whose theory of creative destruction was described in Chapter Three, obtained a law degree from the University of Vienna in 1906. After World War I, Schumpeter briefly served as Minister of Finance in Austria's first republican government. Here he witnessed in hyperinflation, which subsequently led to the rise of fascism in Germany. Being Jewish, he fled Europe in 1932 and moved to Harvard until his death in 1950. While at Harvard, he strongly criticized Keynesian thought. The theory of creative destruction countered the notion of central planning. The most fundamental threat to democracy was seen too be the inflation generated by "well-intentioned" politicians who try to smooth business cycles by increasing welfare payments. Leave the social deviants of capitalism alone.

F. A. Hayek, also first encountered in Chapter Three, studied law and economics at the University of Vienna and obtained his doctorate in 1923. After serving a term in the Austrian Federal Service, he became a lecturer at Vienna from 1929 to 1931. From then until the end of the 1940's, Hayek held a professorship of economic science and statistics at the London School of Economics. Along with his brilliant insights about the useful flows of knowledge in society, Hayek eloquently upheld the ideals of individual liberty. He ridiculed "big government" and the evils of "collectivism". Condemning government agencies and fearing that economic liberalism was leading us down *The Road to Selfdom* (1944).

The Austrians, like the supply siders, favor a full gold standard. But unlike the supply-siders, they want central banks to be totally abolished. Central banks are government controlled monopolies. Instead, let's once again have private banks create their own money, as in the U.S. before the Civil War. Governments must allow people tremendous personal freedom. Taxing wealth punitively and imposing ever-greater restrictions on personal choice is insanity.

Chapter 6

Also expounding Austrian ideas starting in the 1940s was Ayn Rand in New York. *The Fountainhead* (1943) and *Atlas Shrugged* (1957) insisted that selfishness is the moral path, and only capitalism can set the world free. You must be self-sufficient, self-confident and seek objectivism ("akin to libertarianism with a romantic twist"). Most importantly, you must take control of your own destiny; you can't expect the government to take care of you as a benign dictator. In her view, "right" is that which sustains one's own life and "wrong" is that which does not. Her most famous disciple is Alan Greenspan, who received his undergraduate and graduate degrees from New York University, the bastion of Austrian thought in American universities.

Concluding Remarks

You have seen it all—macroeconomics from left to right. You know that most economists have the same well-intentioned objective – to improve living conditions for the masses. How best to do this demonstrates the remarkable array of ideas that "scientists" can formulate. You have to laugh at the myriad of "expert" macroeconomic opinions. No wonder that when one economist says up, another says down. Different attitudes about life guarantee it. But its time to step forward. To forecast the economy, you must pick a particular perspective to analyze all the information input that you are receiving.

APPENDIX 6A

RECIPIENTS OF THE NOBEL PRIZE IN ECONOMIC SCIENCE: 1969-1999

(USA unless otherwise noted)

1969: *RAGNAR FRISCH* (Norway) and *JAN TINBERGEN* (Netherlands) for having developed and applied dynamic models for the analysis of economic processes.

1970: *PAUL A. SAMUELSON* for the scientific work through which he has developed static and dynamic economic theory and actively contributed to raising the level of analysis in economic science.

1971: *SIMON KUZNETS* (USA, Soviet Union) for his empirically founded interpretation of economic growth which has led to new and deepened insight into the economic and social structure and process of development.

1972: *SIR JOHN R. HICKS* (United Kingdom) and *KENNETH J. ARROW* for their pioneering contributions to general economic equilibrium theory and welfare theory.

1973: *WASSILY LEONTIEF* for the development of the input-output method and for its application to important economic problems.

1974: *GUNNAR MYRDAL* (Sweden) and *FRIEDRICH AUGUST VON HAYEK* (Austria, USA) for their pioneering work in the theory of money and economic fluctuations and for their penetrating analysis of the interdependence of economic, social and institutional phenomena.

1975: *LEONID VITALIYEVICH KANTOROVICH* (Soviet Union) and *TJALLING C. KOOPMANS* for their contributions to the theory of optimum allocation of resources.

1976: *MILTON FRIEDMAN* for his achievements in the fields of consumption analysis, monetary history and theory and for his demonstration of the complexity of stabilization policy.

1977: *BERTIL OHLIN* (Sweden) and *JAMES E. MEADE* (United Kingdom) for their pathbreaking contribution to the theory of international trade and international capital movements.

1978: *HERBERT A. SIMON* for his pioneering research into the decision-making process within economic organizations.

1979: *THEODORE W. SCHULTZ* and *SIR ARTHUR LEWIS* (United Kingdom) for their pioneering research into economic development research with particular consideration of the problems of developing countries.

1980: *LAWRENCE R. KLEIN* for the creation of econometric models and the application to the analysis of economic fluctuations and economic policies.

1981: *JAMES TOBIN* for his analysis of financial markets and their relations to expenditure decisions, employment, production and prices.

1982: *GEORGE J. STIGLER* for his seminal studies of industrial structures, functioning of markets and causes and effects of public regulation.

1983: *GERARD DEBREU* for having incorporated new analytical methods into economic theory and for his rigorous reformulation of the theory of general equilibrium.

1984: *SIR RICHARD STONE* (United Kingdom) for having made fundamental contributions to the development of systems of national accounts and hence greatly improved the basis for empirical economic analysis.

1985: *FRANCO MODIGLIANI* (Italy, USA) for his pioneering analyses of saving and of financial markets.

1986: *JAMES M. BUCHANAN, JR.* for his development of the contractual and constitutional bases for the theory of economic and political decision-making.

1987: *ROBERT M. SOLOW* for his contributions to the theory of economic growth.

1988: *MAURICE ALLAIS* (France) for his pioneering contributions to the theory of markets and efficient utilization of resources.

1989: *TRYGVE HAAVELMO* (Norway) for his clarification of the probability theory foundations of econometrics and his analyses of simultaneous economic structures.

1990: *HARRY M. MARKOWITZ, MERTON M. MILLER* and *WILLIAM F. SHARPE* for their pioneering work in the theory of financial economics.

1991: *RONALD H. COASE* (United Kingdom, USA) for his discovery and clarification of the significance of transaction costs and property rights for the institutional structure and functioning of the economy.

1992: *GARY S. BECKER* for having extended the domain of microeconomic analysis to a wide range of human behavior and interaction, including nonmarket behavior.

1993: *ROBERT W. FOGEL* and *DOUGLASS C. NORTH* for having renewed research in economic history by applying economic theory and quantitative methods in order to explain economic and institutional change.

1994: *JOHN C. HARSANYI, JOHN F. NASH* and *REINHARD SELTEN* (Germany)for their pioneering analysis of equilibria in the theory of non-cooperative games.

1995: *ROBERT LUCAS* for having developed and applied the hypothesis of rational expectations, and thereby having transformed macroeconomic analysis and deepened our understanding of economic policy.

1996: *JAMES A. MIRRLEES* (United Kingdom) and *WILLIAM VICKREY* (Canada, USA) for their fundamental contributions to the economic theory of incentives under asymmetric information.

1997: *ROBERT C. MERTON* and *MYRON S. SCHOLES* for a new method to determine the value of derivatives.

1998: *AMARTYA SEN* (India, United Kingdom) for his contributions to welfare economics.

1999: *ROBERT MUNDELL* (Canada, USA) for his analysis of monetary and fiscal policy under different exchange rate regimes and his analysis of optimum currency areas.

APPENDIX 6B

RECIPIENTS OF THE
JOHN BATES CLARK MEDAL: 1947-1999
(Awarded every other year)

Year	Name	Degrees-Where
1947	Paul A. Samuelson	A.B., U. of Chicago, 1935; A.M., Harvard U., 1936; Ph.D., Harvard U., 1941.
1949	Kenneth E. Boulding	B.A., U. of Oxford, 1931; M.A., U. of Oxford, 1939.
1951	Milton Freidman	B.A., Rutgers U., 1932; A.M., U. of Chicago, 1933; Ph.D., Columbia, 1946.
1953	No Award	
1955	James Tobin	A.B., Harvard U., 1939; M.A., Harvard U., 1940; Ph.D., Harvard U., 1947.
1957	Kenneth J. Arrow	B.S., City Coll. Of CUNY, 1940; M.A., Columbia U., 1941; Ph.D., Columbia U., 1951.
1959	Lawrence R. Klein	B.A., U.of Calif., 1942; Ph.D., Mass. Institute of Technology, 1944.
1961	Robert M. Solow	B.A., Harvard U., 1947; M.A., Harvard U., 1949; Ph.D., Harvard U., 1951.
1963	Hendrik S. Houthakker	Ec.Drs., U. of Amsterdam, 1949.

Appendix 6B

1965	Zvi Griliches	B.Sc., U. of Calif., 1953; M.S, U. of Calif., 1954; M.A. U. of Chicago, 1955; Ph.D., U. of Chicago, 1957.
1967	Gary S. Becker	A.B., Princeton U., 1951; A.M. U. of Chicago, 1953; Ph.D., U. of Chicago, 1955.
1969	Marc Leon Nerlove	B.A., U. of Chicago, 1952; M.A., Johns Hopkins U., 1955; Ph.D., Johns Hopkins U., 1956.
1971	Dale W. Jorgenson	B.A., Reed Coll, 1955; A.M., Harvard U., 1957; Ph.D., Harvard U., 1959.
1973	Franklin M. Fisher	A.B., Harvard U., 1956; M.A., Harvard U., 1957; Ph.D., Harvard U., 1960.
1975	Daniel McFadden	B.S., U. of Minn., 1957; Ph.D., U. of Minn., 1962.
1977	Martin S. Feldstein	B.A., Harvard Coll., 1967; D.Phil., Oxford U., 1967.
1979	Joseph E. Stiglitz	B.A., Amherst Coll., 1964; Ph.D., Mass. Institute of Technology, 1966.
1981	A. Michael Spence	B.A., Princeton U., 1966; B.A., Oxford U., 1968; Ph.D., Harvard U., 1972.
1983	James J. Heckman	B.A., Colo. Coll., 1965; M.A., Princeton U., 1968; Ph.D., Princeton U,, 1971; M.A., Yale U., 1989.

1985	Jerry A. Hausman	A.B., Brown U., 1968; B. Phil., U. of Oxford, 1972;D. Phil., U. of Oxford, 1973.
1987	Sanford J. Grossman	B.A., U. of Chicago, 1973; M.A., U. of Chicago, 1974; Ph.D., U. of Chicago, 1975.
1989	David M. Kreps	A.B. Dartmouth Coll., 1972; M.A. Stanford U., 1975; Ph.D. Stanford U.,1975.
1991	Paul R. Krugman	B.A., Yale U., 1974; Ph.D., Mass. Institute of Technology, 1977.
1993	Lawrence H. Summers	S.B., Mass. Institute of Technology, 1975; Ph.D., Harvard U., 1982.
1995	David Card	B.A., Queen's U., 1978; Ph.D., Princeton U., 1983.
1997	Kevin M. Murphy	B.A., U.C.L.A., 1981; Ph.D., U. of Chicago, 1986.
1999	Andrei Sheifer	A.B., Harvard, 1983; Ph.D., Mass. Institute of Technology, 1986.

APPENDIX 6C

CHAIRS OF THE COUNCIL OF ECONOMIC ADVISORS (CEA)

Years served as Chair	Name	Degrees-Where
8/46-11/49	Edwin G. Nourse	A.B. Cornell, 1906; Ph.D, U. of Chicago, 1915.
11/49-1/53	Leon Keyserling	A.B., Columbia U., 1928; LL.B., Harvard U., 1931.
3/53-11/56	Arthur F. Burns	A.B. and A.M., Columbia U., 1925; Ph.D, Columbia U., 1934.
12/56-1/61	Raymond Saulnier	B.S., Middlebury Coll., 1929; M.A., Tufts U., 1931; Ph.D., Columbia U., 1938.
2/61-11/64	Walter Heller	B.A., Oberlin Coll., 1935; M.A., U. of Wisc., 1938; Ph.D., U. of Wisc., 1941.
11/64-2/68	Gardner Ackley	A.B., Western Mich.U., 1936; A.M., U. of Mich., 1937; Ph.D., U. of Mich., 1940.
2/68-1/69	Arthur M. Okun	A.B. Columbia U., 1949; Ph.D. Columbia U., 1956.
2/69-12/71	Paul McCracken	A.B., William Penn Coll., 1937; M.A., Harvard U., 1942; Ph.D., Harvard U., 1948..
1/72-8/74	Herbert Stein	A.B., Williams Coll, 1935; Ph.D., U. of Chicago, 1958.

9/74-1/77	Alan Greenspan	B.S., New York U., 1948; M.A., New York U., 1950; Ph.D., New York U., 1977.
1/77-1/81	Charles Schultze	B.A., Georgetown U., 1948; M.A., Georgetown U., 1950; Ph.D., U. of Md., 1960.
3/81-8/82	Murray Weidenbaum	B.B.A., City Coll. Of CUNY, 1948; M.A., Columbia U., 1949; Ph.D., Princeton U., 1958.
10/82-7/84	Martin Feldstein	B.A., Harvard Coll., 1961; D. Phil., Oxford U., 1967.
4/85-1/89	Beryl Sprinkel	B.S., U. of Mo., 1947; M.B.A., U. of Chicago, 1948; Ph.D., U. of Chicago, 1952.
2/89-1/93	Michael Boskin	B.A., U. of Calif., 1967; M.A., U. of Calif., 1968; Ph.D., U. of Calif. 1971.
2/93-4/95	Laura D'Andrea Tyson	B.A., Smith Coll., 1969; Ph.D., Mass. Institute of Technology, 1974.
6/95-2/97	Joseph Stiglitz	B.A., Amherst Coll. 1964; Ph.D., Mass. Institute of Technology, 1966.
2/97-8/99	Janet Yellen	A.B., Brown U., 1967; Ph.D. Yale U., 1971.
8/99-present	Martin Baily	B.A., Cambridge U., 1966; M.A., Simon Fraser U., 1968; Ph.D., Mass. Institute of Technology, 1972.

Economics is the profession that traditionally
combines the forecasting ability of journeymen
astrologers with the public prestige of the Three Stooges.
—Louis Rukeyser

CHAPTER SEVEN

LOOKING AT THE FUTURE
OF THE U.S. ECONOMY

The failure of macroeconomists to forecast the U.S. economy with consistent accurately is widely recognized and ridiculed. As John Kenneth Galbraith noted "It's not because economists know, but because they are asked."

As a microeconomist, I carefully avoided macroeconomic forecasting in front of large audiences for as long as possible. Then, in 1985, I was asked to be an instructor at the Pacific Coast Banking School. Among the responsibilities was an annual forecasting panel with two other economists, one from the corporate world and one from the banking world. We would make forecasts before leading bankers WHO WOULD BE BACK THE FOLLOWING YEAR. How to avoid total embarrassment? I looked for consistency. This led to four areas.

For a start, what are the major forecasting techniques currently being used and how do they vary in complexity? The jungle thicket demands sharp tools to penetrate its thickness. Then, what school of macroeconomic thought seems most informative in light of the issues on personal outlook raised in Chapter Six. Next, are there basic demographic trends that can be used to see longer-term patterns? Finally, what has been the macroeconomic performance of the U.S. since the end of World War II and the start of the baby boom generation?

After separate presidential administrations are summarized in terms of real GDP growth, inflation, unemployment, interest rates, and money supply growth, my forecast about the U.S. economy over the next ten years is given. Naturally, assumptions have to be made, and such assumptions can cause any forecaster to look like a brilliant sage or a misguided fool. (I would much prefer the former.) Closing comments wrap up the book.

Macroeconomic Forecasting Techniques

Never forget the most basic fact about forecasting. It more *art* than a science. Data are always limited and always tainted or biased. Empirical results come through "filters" to conjure the future from the past. Perspective is unique to each practitioner.

An immediate paradox is that the better you become as an economic forecaster, the more likely you are to be wrong in a *big* way at some point. Many people hop on your bandwagon. Your sheer exposure requires leaps to stay ahead of the mob. You are likely to become convinced of your near infallibility. The longer that you are right, the more dangerous the ride becomes. The balancing nature of life, combined with perceived extreme self-importance, sets you up for a mighty downfall.

To forecast individual series of real GDP growth, inflation, unemployment, and major other macroeconomics indicators of the economy, past values of the variable in question must be examined. Let's begin with the simplest methods.

Mechanical Extrapolation

Mechanical extrapolation is predicting the future value of a variable (mechanistically) from its past values alone. One and two period, no-change forecasts are the most naïve examples. At a higher level is *classical time series analysis*. In this approach, past values can be arranged chronologically and factored/divided into four components: the underlying trend, the cyclical patterns, the seasonal effects, and the residual or error terms. They can be tested for trend, trend-squared, trend-cubed, and trend-to-the-fourth to differentiate linear from nonlinear patterns. Or a ARMA/ARIMA approach may be taken. With such autoregressive-moving average techniques, extrapolaters let the "data do the talking" to find the forecasting equation that best fits the data. It may be a trend line, a sine curve, or whatever. Who knows *a priori?* Unlike classical time series analysis, the data are not subject to preconceived formulas to describe the nature of the data.

Advances in statistical theory since World War II, coupled with the computer revolution and massive amounts of new data, have permitted the technicians and chartists to bend, adjust, filter or massage data with so many procedures that the end result seems so scientific. The equations make it so. But if all you needed were past values of a given variable to predict its future, everyone becomes an accurate forecaster. It's so mechanistic. Yet economic variables often have sharp turning points.

Barometric Techniques

Barometric techniques rely on other variables to signal change in the variable in question. The Conference Board's Index of Leading Indicators (which combines the layoff rate in manufacturing, building permits, plant and equipment spending, crude materials process for an average work week, number of companies receiving slower orders, stock prices, total liquid assets of U.S. companies, the money supply, new factory orders, and the slope of the yield curve on short-term to long-term interest rates) is a broad predictor of the U.S. economy. Of course, many individuals have their own special leading indicators for the economy or certain markets.

Barometric forecasting is a positive step beyond mechanical extrapolation. Major turning points are more likely to be predicted. Even so, we need to diversify our forecasting portfolio further. Let's go directly to the horse's mouth.

Survey or Opinion Polls

This approach polls people directly about the variables in question. For example, the University of Michigan monthly household survey reports on consumer confidence and spending plans, while the National Association of Purchasing

Managers (NAPM) monthly survey reports on delivery times and price pressure.

Perhaps the best-known opinion poll of macroeconomic variables is the *Blue Chip Survey* of 52 top forecasting entities (banks, universities, private firms, and private consultants) from across the country each month. These firms are surveyed about a series of variables, and group averages are determined for real GDP growth, the GDP deflator, nominal GDP growth, the consumer price index, industrial production, real disposable personal income, real personal consumption expenditures, real-non-residential fixed investment, current corporate profits, the average yearly rates for 3-month Treasury bills and 10-year Treasury notes, the civilian unemployment rate, total annual housing starts, total annual auto/truck sales, and total real-net exports. The idea here is quite simple: there is safety in numbers when polling "experts."

Certainly, economic surveys like these broaden our understanding of the U.S. economy and particular markets. But an obvious problem with any survey or opinion poll is the tremendous faith being placed in the respondents to give accurate, thoughtful or truthful answers. What if they are "gaming" or giving false answers? A second problem is costs. Good surveys are not cheap to conduct, and they can become especially expensive to update.

Econometric Modeling

For professional economists, the most elegant, the most sophisticated, and the most complete forecasting technique is *econometric modeling*. Here, economic theory serves as a guide to the data and then formal statistical techniques are applied for quantification. The end-result may be a simple one-equation model, as when estimating a market demand curve. Or it may be a two-equation, three-equation, or multi-equation model. The data may be either times series, or cross-sectional and the numbers may be obtained through surveys, reports, or personal observations.

The highest level of complexity and sophistication is found in the massive macro models that contain hundreds, *even thousands*, of variables and hundreds of equations. The possible number of interactions are enormous. Dependent variables in one set of equations become independent variables in another set. Specifying them is a daunting task.

Nonetheless, once they are properly specified, econometric models yield precise numerical values. They quantify the magnitude of turning points. Simulation games can be conducted. In essence, they capture the best features of the other three forecasting techniques.

Even with their wondrous mathematical sophistication, models of the economy are not relied upon 100 percent. When major forecasters are asked what percent of their final forecast is judgment or opinion as opposed to the actual numbers generated by the computer, their typical response is around 40 to 50 percent. Think of it! After all the countless hours of deciding which theoretical equations to include, of gathering and massaging the necessary data, and of finally generating results with the most advanced statistical methods, major forecasters still rely upon their intuition and "feel of the market." No wonder the macro forecasting crowd takes on the appearance of journeymen astrologers. If I were one of the Three Stooges, I'd sue Louis Rukeyser for slander.

How Economics Has Convinced Me

Of course I accept that marginalism, opportunity costs, diminishing physical returns lead to the inescapable fact of scarcity. The laws of demand and supply are always present to bring conflicting desires into balance. Distortions of all sorts are possible in the marketplace, but individual markets have many self-correcting qualities that ultimately benefit the majority of consumers if left "unregulated."

Modern economics is not the study of common sense, given its many complexities and paradoxes, nor is it the study of how to make everybody happy. It's about trade-offs of individual freedoms among consumers and producers. It's about getting the most out of situations given the binding constraints at hand. Fundamentally, it comes down to the will to improve over the inertia of the status quo.

The most arrogant of all economic beliefs is the idea that wage and price controls benefit the majority of consumers. To think that a group of "very smart" individuals knows more about prices and output than the collective market wisdom of thousands (millions, billions) of individual traders is incredible. Likewise, to believe that the U.S. government should engage actively in "industrial policy," trying to subsidize what it considers leading-edge firms of the economy, demonstrates overbearing pride.

Instead, I put faith in the ability and ingenuity of individuals operating "freely" under a variety of market structures. Let them determine what is "best" in the broad social sense, not select social engineers. As Edgar Allen noted, "I have great faith in fools; self-confidence, my friends call it."

Generally speaking, free-market economists are not an especially envious group. Efficiency rather than equity is the battle cry when confronting markets. Indeed, many economists accept the notion of *Pareto optimal*, whereby making one or more persons better off without making others worse off must improve social welfare.

As a group, free marketeers also espouse differentiation and diversity. Marginalism creates an appreciation for the special differences and the little things in life. Homogeneity may help generate a theoretically ideal market, but the forces of creative destructive and evermore improved consumer products best describe the U.S. economy.

Having worked as an assistant manager at a bowling alley while a graduate student at Duke, I am forced to reject rational expectations for the majority of the human race. People can be fooled systematically in the short run. Speculative bubbles can develop. Instead the macro school that I find most insightful is monetarism. Friedman puts the story together better than any other economist that I have read or met. Each week, as soon as the *U.S. Financial Data* from the Federal Reserve Bank of St. Louis comes, I immediately turn to the page on M_2 to see what its growth rate is over the past year, the past six months, and the past three months. Anything over six percent and I'm really worried about inflation. I also look at the growth rates for the adjusted monetary base, MZM, and M_1 for clues.

For more technical understanding of the differing growth rates relative to Fed policy, I read the monthly publication *Economics Trends* of the Federal Reserve Bank of Cleveland, the *Wall Street Journal*, and professional journals. We monetarists can never lose sight of monetary policy (or, for that matter, fiscal policy).

U.S. Demographic Patterns in Relation to the Economy

Demographic patterns are an invaluable component of my macro forecasts. Not only can the size of various age groups be predicted well into the future, economists have also developed models of lifetime consumption behavior that then anticipate spending and saving plans for decades to come.

Working Age Groups and Inflation

Table 7.1 presents the percent of the population by age groups for census years since 1940. For instance, in 1940, eight percent of the U.S. population was under 5 years of age, and another 17 percent was between 5 and 14. Also shown in Table 7.1 are the percentage changes over each decade in the three adult working age groups, 20-24, 25-39, and 40-64. These groups hold a key to inflation.

The 20-24 year-old and 25-39 year-old populations are typically debtors, individuals who favor easy money and inflation. The 40-64 year-olds, in contrast, have more financial wealth to protect thus favor sound money (low money growth). Now suppose inflation by decade with these demographics alone? Let's start with the 1940's.

This decade saw a slight decline in the 20-24 year olds, a healthy increase in the 25-39 year-old population, and an even healthier increase in the 40-64 year olds. Without the war, demographic patterns would have favored a sound money environment. However, financing the war efforts meant the Fed kept keeping nominal interest rates low for the U.S. Treasury. So M_2 grew 13+ percent each year from 1941 to 1945, and 9 percent in 1946. Even with price controls, coupons for key commodities, and the sales of war bonds to soak up disposable income, this rapid money growth created double digit inflation throughout the war years. After the war ended, M_2 grew less than 2 percent form 1947 to 1950.

Table 7.1: U.S. Age Proportions and Adult Population Percentage Changes: 1940-2000

Age Group	1940		1950		1960		1970		1980		1990		2000
< 5	8		11		11		9		7		7		8
5-14	17		16		20		20		15		14		14
15-19	9		7		7		9		9		7		7
20-24	9	-1	8	-6	6	51	8	30	9	-13	7	-6	7	11
25-39	22	13	23	0.4	20	3	18	42	23	25	26	-8	22	-6
40-64	27	17	27	16	27	13	26	4	24	15	26	29	31	17
65-74	5		5		6		6		7		7		7
75+	3		3		3		4		5		5		6
Decade Growth Rate		14		19		13		11		10		7		5
Median Age	29.0		30.2		29.5		27.9		30.0		33.0		35.7

Source: U.S. Census Bureau *Abstracts* (various years); Current Population Reports *Projections of the Population of the United States by Age, Sex, and Race: 1990-2080* (Series P-25, No.1018, 1989).

The 1950's saw a further decline in the 20-24 year-old population due to the low birth rates of the later 1920's and early 1930's. A slight increase in the 25-39 year-old population occurred, and the double-digit increase in the 40-64 year-old population continued. The demographic patterns in the 1950's signaled for an even sounder money environment than the 1940's. Subsequently, the growth in M_2 growth averaged less than 4 percent a year from 1950 to 1959.

The 1960's saw baby boomers, born between 1946 and 1964, becoming young adults. The 20-24 year old population exploded 51 percent! In contrast, the 25-39 population increased only 3 percent and the 40-64 year-old population growth rate slowed to 13 percent. The demographic winds were now shifting towards easier money. Except for 4 percent growth in 1966, M_2 growth was over 7 percent every year from 1961 through 1968. Financing the Viet Nam war kept M_2 growth over 8 percent the last two years of the Johnson Administration. Inflation rates headed strongly upward.

The 1970's witnessed massive explosions in both the 20-24 and 25-39 populations. On the other hand, the 40-64 population growth rate fell to just 4 percent. What an environment for easy money! The growth in M_2 growth averaged nearly ten percent a year from 1970 through 1979. Annual double-digit inflation occurred twice.

The 1980's continued to have a sharp expansion of the 25-39 population as baby boomers moved through these years. However, the 20-24 year-old population, the Generation X'ers born between 1965 and 1976, declined 13 percent, while the 40-64 population tripled to 15 percent growth. The winds were shifting back toward sound money. M_2 growth averaged over 8 percent between 1980 and 1987, but only 3 percent 1987-89. Inflation hovered in the 3-5 percent range.

In the 1990's, both the 20-24 and 25-39 populations declined more than 6 percent. In contrast, the 40-64 year old population grew at 29 percent, twice the rate of the 1980's. The demographic winds couldn't have been blowing more forcefully in favor of sound money. Certainly the Fed under Alan Greenspan's leadership has done a marvelous job since the later 1980's. But keep in mind that it has operated in a highly favorable demographic environment.

As for the first decade of the new millennium, while there will be 11 percent growth in the 20-24 year-old population, the 25-39 population is expected to decline 6 percent. The 40-64 population growth will fall, but still be at 17 percent. From a strictly demographic perspective, it looks like another sound money environment.

The Fifty-and-Older Population

Table 7.2 examines the U.S. population 50-and-older from 1990 until 2040. Remarkably, 26 percent of the U.S. population was 50+ in 1990, well before the first of the baby boomers turned 50. By 2020, nearly 40 percent of the population is projected to be 50+.

It is important to take note of the varying growth rates by decade across the three subgroups listed: 50-64 (the "young old"), 65-79 ("retirees"), and 80+ (the "elderly", two-thirds of whom are women). The differences in growth patterns among the three subgroups are critical for many firms, industries, and government agencies as they make revenue and service projections over the next several decades. The bulges in particular age groups create dynamic planning issues for retirement-driven communities and states.

Table 7.2: Propotions of the Total Population and Percentage Changes in Older age Groups in the U.S.: 1990-2040

Year	Age Group	Proportion of Total Population	Age Group	Percentage Change over The Decade
1990	50+	26%	50-64	26%
	65+	13%	65-79	4%
	80+	3%	80+	32%
			U.S. POP.	7%
2000	50+	28%	50-64	38%
	65+	13%	65-79	10%
	80+	3%	80+	22%
			U.S. POP.	5%
2010	50+	34%	50-64	5%
	65+	14%	65-79	32%
	80+	4%	80+	6%
			U.S. POP.	4%
2020	50+	38%	50-64	-12%
	65+	18%	65-79	23%
	80+	4%	80+	37%
			U.S. POP.	2%
2030	50+	39%	50-64	5%
	65+	22%	65-79	-8%
	80+	6%	80+	49%
			U.S. POP.	4%

Source: Population Projections of the United States by Age, Sex, Race and Hispanic Origin: 1995-2050. Current Population Reports, Middle Series, Population Estimates and Projections, Series P-25, No. 1030, February, 1996.

Three "Generations" Since 1946

Generational age-groupings are quite common as social scientists and the public consider prevailing attitudes and future economic patterns. Three "generations" in the U.S. since 1946 are:

- **The Baby-Boom Generation.** Between the start of 1946 and the end of 1964, 77 million U.S. births occurred, and they fell on a population of some 140 million. No wonder this generation is portrayed as a pig moving through a boa constrictor. Baby boomers were reared as the "chosen" and the "special," the first TV generation. They were told they can "change the world" if they put their minds to it. At the moment, baby-boomers range in age form 36 to 54. Most of us have no expectations of dying for quite some time!

- **Generation X.** Between the start of 1965 when annual births began to decline significantly (267,000 births), to the end of 1976, when annual births began to increase significantly (159,00 births), slightly over 41 million U.S. births occurred. They were the first "latch-key" kids, where often both parents worked, plus they lived through the sharp jump in divorce rates. Accordingly, as a group they are often portrayed as independent, tough, cynical, and the "grunge" crowd. At the moment, generation X'ers range in age from 24 to 36.

- **Generation Y or the Rainbow Generation.** Between the start of 1977 and the end of 1995, nearly 72 million births occurred. This is almost the same absolute size as the baby-boom generation, although it occurred on a much larger population base. This is a generation immersed by split-households and single parents. They have been strongly influenced by arguments for cultural diversity and are seemingly more self-assured that generation X'ers. Y'ers are the first generation to grow-up with personal computers. They are also the first U.S. generation this century not to live through a war or sharp economic decline. Surveys indicate that they generally respect authority, like their parents, and want good-paying jobs when they graduate from school. At the moment, generation Y'ers range in age from 5 to 23.

Harry Dent's Demographic Viewpoint

Harry Dent Jr., first in the *Great Boom Ahead* (1993) and then in *The Roaring 2000's* (1998), relied primarily on demographics to forecast a boom until 2008. Americans in the 44-50 age bracket, with high discretionary income and a relatively long time before retirement, are seen as the driving consumer force for the economy. Their spending actions, savings behavior, and stock investments are the keys to understanding what will happen to 2008.

Figure 7.1: Average Annual Family Spending by Age
(5-year age groups)

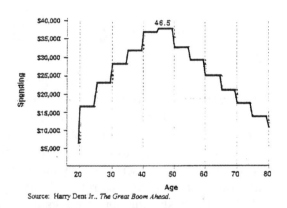

Source: Harry Dent Jr., *The Great Boom Ahead.*

Dent found that family spending peaks at age 46.5, as seen in Figure 7.1, and then Figure 7.2 shows his key picture: U.S. births lagged 44-46 years (with an adjustment for 25 year olds) plotted against the S&P 500 Index. According to Dent, spending is more fundamental than saving in driving financial markets. "Bull markets can't continue without economic growth and rising earnings. The stock market's primary function is to value the future earnings of stocks. At the same time, the flow of funds from savings can significantly affect the valuations of the market relative to the growing earnings trends through the increased supply of funds chasing fewer stocks".

Figure 7.2: The Spending Wave: 44-46 Ywar Birth Lag (Includes 25% of Change in 25-Ywar Olds)

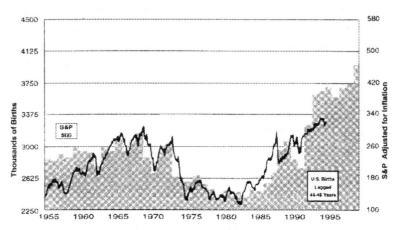

Since baby boomers will be moving through the 44-50 age bracket in full force until 2008, Dent predicts strong growth for the U.S. economy and the Dow Index is in the range of 19,00 to 36,000 by 2008. Then the demographic outlook changes. The growth of national spending and firms' earnings will slow because the last of the baby boomers turns 44. Moreover, the oldest of the baby boomers will start to retire. Dent argues that investors will likely begin shifting out of stocks into bonds and other fixed income assets as they move into retirement. As a result, bonds will do much better than stocks after 2008. Stock prices may even come tumbling down due to less national spending as X'ers now supplant boomers in the peak years of 44-56.

The U.S. Economy and Presidential Administrations Since 1946

To judge the performance of an economy, a scorecard is found in Table 7.3. It provides nine official government series since 1946, reported form the 1988 and 2000 *Economic Reports of the President*.

Real GDP (GNP) growth, as we saw in Chapter Five, is the primary measure by which economists judge improvements in living conditions and the wealth of nations. For the past hundred years, real GDP growth has averaged approximately 3 percent, but it is closer to 4 percent if the Great Depression is left out. Anything above 4 percent growth for extended periods causes delirium among U.S. macroeconomists.

Two prices indexes are given, the GDP (GNP) deflator in 1996 dollars and the CPI in 1982-84 dollars. The GDP deflator averaged close to zero from the 1870's to 1940, whereas it has averaged nearly five percent since. The CPI is a post- WWII index and has averaged 4.4 percent from 1946 to the present.

The unemployment rate looks only at the civilian labor force. It has averaged 5.5 percent over the past century.

The financial variables are the nominal yields on AAA corporate bonds and two measures of the money supply: M_1 (currency held by the nonbank public, demand deposits, other checkable deposits, and travelers checks), and M_2 (M_1 plus savings accounts including money market deposit accounts, small time deposits under $100,000, and retail money funds).

Chapter 7

Table 7.3: Annual Data on the Macroeconomic Performance of the U.S.: 1946-1999

Year Or GDP	Real GDP (GNP) Growth	GDP (GNP) Deflator%* (1996 Dollars)	CPI%* (1982-84)	Unemployment Rate (Civilian)	Average AAA Bond Rate	M$_1$%**	M$_2$%**	Surplus/ Deficit% of GPD (GNP)	Exports % of GDP (GNP)
1946	-19.0	22.9	8.3	3.9	2.53	6.6	9.1	-7.5	7.2
47	-2.8	13.9	14.4	3.9	2.61	4.8	0.6	-1.8	8.6
48	3.9	7.0	8.1	3.8	2.82	0.2	1.5	4.8	6.7
49	0.0	-0.5	-1.2	5.9	2.66	-0.9	-0.5	0.2	6.3
1950	8.5	2.0	1.3	5.3	2.62	2.9	2.3	-1.2	5.0
51	10.3	4.8	7.9	3.3	2.86	4.5	3.7	1.9	5.9
52	3.9	1.5	1.9	3.0	2.96	4.9	5.4	-0.4	5.5
53	4.0	1.6	0.8	2.9	3.20	2.4	3.8	-1.8	4.5
54	-1.3	1.6	0.7	5.5	2.90	1.6	3.5	-0.3	5.0
55	5.6	3.2	-0.4	4.4	3.06	3.2	3.7	-0.8	5.2
56	2.1	3.4	1.5	4.1	3.36	1.1	1.7	0.9	5.9
57	1.7	3.6	3.3	4.3	3.89	0.4	2.6	0.8	6.3
58	-0.8	2.1	2.8	6.8	3.79	1.4	4.9	-0.6	5.3
59	5.8	1.0	0.7	5.5	4.38	3.9	5.8	-2.7	5.0
1960	2.5	1.4	1.7	5.5	4.41	0.5	4.9	0.1	5.8
61	2.3	1.1	1.0	6.7	4.35	3.2	7.4	-0.6	4.8
62	6.0	1.4	1.0	5.5	4.33	1.8	8.1	-1.3	4.7
63	4.3	1.1	1.3	5.7	4.26	3.7	8.4	-0.8	4.8
64	5.8	1.5	1.3	5.2	4.40	4.6	8.0	-0.9	5.1
65	6.4	1.9	1.6	4.5	4.49	4.7	8.1	-0.2	4.9
66	6.6	2.9	2.9	3.8	5.13	2.5	4.6	-0.5	4.9
67	2.5	3.1	3.1	3.8	5.51	6.5	9.3	-1.1	5.0
68	4.8	4.3	4.2	3.6	6.18	7.7	8.0	-2.9	5.0
69	3.1	4.8	5.5	3.5	7.03	3.3	3.7	0.3	5.0
1970	0.2	5.3	5.7	4.9	8.04	5.1	6.6	-0.3	5.5
71	3.1	5.3	4.4	5.9	7.39	6.5	13.4	-2.1	5.3
72	5.3	4.4	3.2	5.6	7.21	9.2	13.0	-2.0	5.4
73	5.7	5.7	6.2	4.9	7.44	5.5	6.6	-1.1	6.6
74	-0.3	8.6	11.0	5.6	8.56	4.3	5.5	-0.4	8.3
75	-0.3	9.2	9.1	8.5	8.83	4.7	12.7	-3.4	8.4
76	5.2	6.0	5.8	7.7	8.43	6.7	13.4	-4.2	8.2
77	4.5	6.5	6.5	7.1	8.02	8.1	10.3	-2.7	7.8
78	5.7	6.9	7.6	6.1	8.73	8.0	7.5	-2.7	8.1
79	3.4	8.1	11.3	5.8	9.63	6.9	7.9	-1.6	8.9
1980	0.0	8.9	13.5	7.1	11.94	6.9	8.5	-2.7	10.0
81	2.5	9.3	10.3	7.6	14.71	6.9	9.7	-2.6	9.7
82	-1.9	6.1	6.2	9.7	13.79	8.7	8.8	-4.0	8.7
83	4.2	4.1	3.2	9.6	12.04	9.8	11.3	-6.0	7.9
84	7.3	3.7	4.3	7.5	12.17	5.8	8.6	-4.8	7.8
85	3.9	3.1	3.6	7.2	11.37	12.4	8.0	-5.1	7.2
86	3.4	2.2	1.9	7.0	9.02	16.9	9.5	-5.0	7.3
87	3.5	2.9	3.6	6.2	9.38	3.5	3.6	-3.2	7.8
88	4.2	3.4	4.1	5.5	9.71	4.9	5.8	-3.1	8.9
89	3.5	3.9	4.8	5.3	9.26	0.8	5.5	-2.8	9.4
1990	1.7	3.9	5.4	5.6	9.32	4.0	3.8	-3.9	9.7
91	-0.2	3.4	4.2	6.8	8.77	8.7	3.1	-4.5	10.2
92	3.3	2.2	3.0	7.5	8.14	14.3	1.6	-4.7	10.2
93	2.4	2.7	3.0	6.9	7.22	10.2	1.6	-3.9	10.0
94	4.0	2.1	2.6	6.1	7.97	1.8	0.4	-2.9	10.4
95	2.7	2.1	2.8	5.6	7.59	2.0	4.2	-2.2	11.1
96	3.7	1.8	3.0	5.4	7.37	-4.0	4.8	-1.4	11.4
97	4.5	1.7	2.3	4.9	7.26	-0.6	5.8	-0.3	11.7
98	4.3	1.2	1.6	4.5	6.53	1.7	8.8	0.8	11.0
99***	4.0	1.5	2.2	4.2	7.04	2.9	5.9	1.4	10.8

*The 2000 *Economic Report of the President* only provides GDP values from 1959 onward. Here 1996 is the base year for the GDP deflator and 1982-84 is the base year in the CPI. The 1988 *Economic Report of the President* provides the 1946 to 1959 values for real GNP growth, the GNP deflator (in 1967 dollars).
**The *Economic Report of the President* do not provide values on M$_1$ and M$_2$ prior to 1960. *The American Business Cycle: Continuity and Change*, Robert Gordon, ed., 1986, provides M$_1$ and M$_2$ values for 1946 to 1960.
***Provisional numbers.

Completing the statistics are the federal government surpluses or deficits as a percent of nominal GDP (GNP) and U.S. exports as a percent of nominal GDP (GNP).

Averages Since 1946

The averages for the first seven variables from 1946 to 1999 are:

Real GDP (GNP) Growth	3.0%
GDP (GNP) Deflator	4.3%
CPI	4.3%
Unemployment Rate	5.8%
AAA Bond Rate	7.1%
M_1 Growth	4.9%
M_2 Growth	6.2%

Deficits of at least two percent of GDP became common in the early 1970's after smaller percentages in the 1940's, 1950, and 1960's. The level of exports as a percent of GDP began to move up noticeably after the mid-1970's and have risen to over 10 percent in the 1990's due to NAFTA, GATT and other free trade initiatives. Let's now consider the presidential administrations and their overall economic grades.

Truman Years: 1946-1952

Economic Scorecard (Averages)

Real GNP Growth ('82 base)	.7	(5.3 after '47)
GNP Deflator ('82)	7.4	(3.0 after '47)
CPI ('67)	5.8	(3.6 after '47)
Unemployment Rate	4.2	
AAA Bond Rate	2.7	
M_1 Growth	3.8	
M_2 Growth	3.7	

Major Economic Players

Fed Chairs

Marriner Eccles	(4/'39-4/'48)
Thomas McCabe	(4/'48-3/'51)
William Martin, Jr.	(4/'51-1/'70)

CEA Chairs

| Edwin Nourse | (8/'46-11/'49) |
| Leon Keyserling | (11/'49-1/'53) |

Key Features:

- Many people anticipated another major recession/depression after WWII due to the sharp drop in government spending. While real growth plummeted in 1946, it had rebounded by 1948. The Employment Act of 1946 seemed to help. U.S. firms quickly converted from wartime to peacetime production.
- The GI Bill of Rights, passed in 1944, ignited the postwar college boom starting in 1946. It created significant demand for higher education and helped create a higher quality work force. In the process, it also served as a very effective riot control measure for returning soldiers who had been blasting away in Europe and the Asian Pacific. It opened up American universities and colleges to all classes of society, not just the well-to-do.
- Strong inflation in 1948 turned to deflation in 1949. Tight monetary policy starting in 1947 played a critical role.
- Consumer prices exploded in 1951. Households, seeing the Korean War build-up, bought in a frenzy in anticipation of rationing and long lines like during World War II.
- Nominal interest rates remained extremely low due to government credit controls and the Fed being under the U.S. Treasury's influence until 1951. Then, even though Truman fought the Fed-Treasury separation in 1951, Eccles favored it, and the Fed was finally given its independence from the U.S. Treasury.
- Overall Economic Grade: A-, had strong GNP growth starting in 1947, fairly low unemployment, and very low interest rates.

Eisenhower Years: 1953-1960

Economic Scorecard (Averages)

Real GNP Growth ('82 base)	2.5
GNP Deflator ('82)	2.4

CPI ('67)	1.7
Unemployment Rate	4.9
AAA Bond Rate	3.6
M_1 Growth	1.8
M_2 Growth	3.9
Major Economic Players	
Fed Chairs	
William Martin, Jr.	(4/'51-1/'70)
CEA Chairs	
Arthur Burns	(3/'53-12/'56)
Raymond Saulnier	(12/'56-1/'61)

Key Features:

- Real GNP growth was below the 100-year average for the Eisenhower years even though the U.S. was the economic colossus of the world. Powerful oligopolies and labor unions caused distortions. While it was "happy days" for the white middle-class, minorities continued to suffer economically and socially.
- Recessions occurred in 1954 and 1957-58, but the economy rebounded strongly the following year.
- 1955 was the last time that one of the price indexes actually registered deflation for an entire year.
- American Keynesians defined full employment as a 4 percent unemployment rate, so the "high" rates at the end of the decade caused growing concern among the MIT-Harvard-Washington, D.C. liberal crowd.
- Eisenhower wasn't able to vigorously campaign for Nixon as President in 1960 due to poor health. Nixon would later place much blame on the Fed and it's tight monetary policies for his election defeat by Kennedy.
- Overall Economic Grade: B, had moderate growth, okay unemployment numbers, and good inflation numbers.

Kennedy-Johnson Years: 1961-1968

Economic Scorecard (Averages)

Real GDP Growth ('96 base)	4.8

GDP Deflator ('96)	2.2
CPI ('82-84)	2.1
Unemployment Rate	4.9
AAA Bond Rate	4.8
M_1 Growth	4.3
M_2 Growth	7.7

Major Economic Players
  Fed Chairs
    William Martin, Jr.   (4/'51-1/'70)
  CEA Chairs
    Walter Heller   (1/'61-11/'64)
    Gardner Ackley   (11/'64-2/'68)
    Arthur Okun   (2/'68-1/'69)

Key Features

- The relatively high unemployment rates in Kennedy's first two years led Heller and other Keynesian advisers to argue for a significant income tax cut.
- The 1964 income tax cut apparently created a great boom and convinced American Keynesians that they could "fine tune" the U.S. economy. The Keynesian revolution reaches its peak influence from 1965 to 1969.
- Johnson wanted a Great Society, but he also chose to fight the Vietnam war. Since the economy was at full employment, it was the classic trade-off of guns versus butter, and something had to give. No wonder he pleaded for more one-armed economists!
- The Fed under Martin monetarized government deficits in 1967-68, pushing up the growth rates in M_1 and M_2. The rate of inflation accelerated.
- 1961-1969 was, until recently, the longest economic expansion in U.S. history approximately 106 months in length. It was Camelot to economic liberals.
- Overall Economic Grade: B+, had amazing numbers on growth and unemployment, but increasingly lost touch with the long-run realities of a *laissez-faire* marketplace.

Nixon-Ford Years: 1969-1976
Economic Scorecard (Averages)

Real GDP Growth ('96 base)	2.8
GDP Deflator ('96)	6.1
CPI ('82-84)	6.4
Unemployment Rate	5.8
AAA Bond Rate	7.9
M_1 Growth	5.7
M_2 Growth	9.0

Major Economic Players
Fed Chairs

William Martin, Jr.	(4/'51-1/'70)
Arthur Burns	(2/'70-2/'78)

CEA Chairs

Paul McCracken	(2/'69-12/'71)
Herbert Stein	(1/'72-8/'74)
Alan Greenspan	(9/'74-1/'77)

Key Features:
* Nixon and Martin agree to slow the growth rate in M_1 and M_2 in 1969 in order to reduce inflation.
* Stagflation appears in 1970, causing the Nixon administration to adopt price controls in 1971. The last of the price controls aren't repealed until 1974.
* Nixon strongly encourages Burns to follow an expansionary monetary policy as the 1972 presidential election approaches. The result is a quick boom, and Nixon rides to victory in a landslide (as if that's any real surprise given that George McGovern was the Democratic nominee).
* Long lines to purchase gasoline occur in many parts of the country in 1973 due to OPEC, the oil embargo, and gasoline price controls. This is another classic attempt by the federal government to set prices that ultimately results in long lines, black markets, and poorer service.
* Both the economy and Nixon go into the tank in 1974. The president is forced to resign and is replaced by Gerald Ford

(who, some argued, played one too many football games without a helmet on). The economy is experiencing double-digit inflation and negative GDP growth—nice job Dick!

- Budget deficits as a percent of GDP jump significantly in 1975 and 1976.
- By 1976, real GDP growth is over 5 percent, both price indexes have fallen significantly from the previous year, and the unemployment rate is headed back down even though baby boomers are flooding the labor market. Thank goodness for Alan Greenspan.
- Overall Economic Grade: C, if not for the work of Alan Greenspan, it would be an F, especially if awarded in 1974.

Carter Years: 1977-1980

Economic Scorecard (Averages)

Real GDP Growth ('96 base)	3.4
GDP Deflator ('96)	7.6
CPI ('82-84)	9.7
Unemployment Rate	9.5
AAA Bond Rate	9.6
M_1 Growth	7.5
M_2 Growth	8.6

Major Economic Players

Fed Chairs

Arthur Burns	(2/'70-2/'78)
G. William Miller	(3/'78-7/'79)
Paul Volcker	(8/'79-8/'87)

CEA Chair

Charles Schultze	(1/'77-1/'81)

Key Features:

- In the 1976 presidential election debates, Carter argued that the fundamental economic problem facing the U.S. was unemployment, while Ford said the problem was inflation. After his victory, Carter and his Keynesian advisors were determined to push the unemployment rate down.

- Tremendous upheaval occurred in labor markets as young adult baby boomers flooded into the economy along. Sharp increases in female labor force participation rates become particularly noticeable. The full employment rate was argued by conservatives to be greater than the four percent unemployment definition of the Keynesians in the 1950's and 1960's.
- The rapid growth in M_2, first by Burns in 1976 and 1977, then by G. William Miller in 1978 and 1979, stoked inflationary fires. The price of gold explodes to over $800 an ounce.
- Carter viewed the energy crisis as the "moral equivalent of war", (certainly the case if you try to fight the laws of demand and supply with price controls).
- Strong real GDP growth occurred in 1977 and 1978, moderated in 1979, and then the really fell out in 1980.
- The Fed targeted the growth in M_1 in late 1979 after Paul Volcker becomes Chair. This dooms Carter's chance for re-election with rapidly rising interest rates.
- Deregulation of transportation, communications, and banking industries takes place.
- Overall Economic Grade: C+, had strong growth until last year when inflation became ugly and the economy weakened, deregulation was a positive force for the future, but again Keynesian advisers were mortgaging the future for the present.

Reagan Years: 1981-1988
Economic Scorecard (Averages)

Real GDP Growth ('96 base)	3.4	(4.4 after the 81-82 recession)
GDP Deflator ('96)	4.4	(3.5 after the 81-82 recession)
CPI ('82-84)	4.7	
Unemployment Rate	7.5	
M_1 Growth	8.7	
M_2 Growth	8.2	

Major Economic Players

Chapter 7

Fed Chairs
    Paul Volcker   (8/'79-8/'87)
    Alan Greenspan   (9/'87-present)
CEA Chairs
    Murray Weidenbaum   (2/'81-8/'82)
    Martin Feldstein   (10/'80-7/'84)
    Beryl Sprinkel   (4/'85-1/'89)

Key Features:

- Tighter monetary policy by Volcker and the Fed meant sharply rising interest rates through 1981 (the prime rate hits 20%). In 1981-82 the U.S. economy experiences the worse downturn since the Great Depression.
- Reagan's income tax cuts, without accompanying cuts in federal spending, create the greatest deficits in U.S. history. The national debt more than doubled during Reagan's first four years in office.
- Deregulation of financial markets in 1980 apparently impacted the relationship between M_2 growth and the inflation indices. Inflation fell sharply from 1981 to 1986 even though M_2 growth averaged over 9 percent form 1981-86.
- 1984 was a marvelous year for Americans and the Reagan administration. Growth was 7 percent and the unemployment rate fell sharply. In addition, the East Germans, Cubans, and Russians did not show up at the L.A. Olympic Games, so the U.S. wins 83 gold medals. Reagan's Star Wars plan is impacting the Soviet Union. An actor who used to make movies with chimpanzees becomes a resounding cheerleader for capitalism!
- At the same time, the Democrats go into a dark room, muddle about, and decide to nominate Walter Mondale for president, who, if elected, will raise tax rates!
- Rapid monetary growth finally caused the price indexes to move upward in 1987.
- Volcker resigns in August, 1987, as Chair of the Fed. His inflation legacy is diminished by U.S. Treasury attempts to devalue the U.S. dollar to reduce trade deficits.

- Tight monetary policy ensured in 1987 as Greenspan became Chair of the Fed. Just two months after taking office, he faced the October '87 stock market crash. The Fed withstands the storm by serving as the lender of last resort. The economy rebounded with strong growth in 1988, contrary to the major downturn boom many doomsdayers expected.
- Until recently, the Reagan boom, which started in November 1982, and lasted 92 months, was the longest peacetime expansion in U.S. history.
- Overall Economic Grade: B+, strong kudos for Reagan's optimism, love of democracy and capitalism, and the job engine he unleashed through supply-side tax cuts, but the deficit problem lingered and U.S. Treasury policy under James Baker was weak after 1984.

Bush Years: 1989-1992

Economic Scorecard (Averages)

Real GDP Growth ('96)	2.1
GDP Deflator ('96)	3.4
CPI ('82-84)	4.4
Unemployment Rate	6.3
AAA Bond Rate	8.9
M_1 Growth	7.0
M_2 Growth	3.5

Major Economic Players

Fed Chair

    Alan Greenspan   (8/'87-present)

CEA Chair

    Michael Boskin   (2/'89-1/'93)

Key Features:

- Bush's promise, "Read my lips, no new taxes!" translated into a major federal tax increase in 1990.
- Even highly favorable demographics, an extensive free-trade environment, the fall of the Communist empire, and a 24-hour war victory over the Iraqis couldn't prevent a recession from July, 1990, to March, 1991.

- Rather than reducing regulatory burdens, the Bush Administration extended federal rules and red tape in many parts of the economy.
- Bush and his Secretary of the Treasury Nicholas Brady had no understanding of Reaganomics. They gave new meaning to the phrase "lost in time and space!" in the macroeconomic jungle.
- Overall Economic Grade: D+, had a group of clowns in the Executive Branch who obviously lost their understanding free-market capitalism.

Clinton Years: 1993-200

Economic Scorecard (Averages)

Real GDP Growth ('96 base)	3.7
GDP Deflator ('96)	1.5
CPI ('82-84)	2.5
Unemployment Rate	5.4
AAA Bond Rate	7.3
M_1 Growth	2.0
M_2 Growth	4.5

Major Economic Players

Fed Chair

Alan Greenspan (8/'87-present)

CEA Chairs

Laura D'Andrea Tyson	(2/'93-4/'95)
Joseph Stiglitz	(6/'95-2/'97)
Janet Yellen	(2/'97-8/'99)
Martin Baily	(8/'99-present)

Key Features:

- The Clinton Administration tried to "manage" the health care industry upon taking office and was a total failure.
- The economic team surrounding Clinton continues to be dominated by MIT- educated economists. Thank heaven for Alan Greenspan as a conservative counterweight.
- More government red tape and regulation has risen for small businesses than occurred during the Bush administration.

- Personal scandal and impeachment threatened the Clinton Administration in 1998, but the booming economy worked strangely in his favor. The U.S. has just achieved its longest economic expansion—108 months —and is still rolling along.
- Overall Economic Grade: B, in large because Clinton had enough sense to spare the economy form liberal Democratic prescriptions and to listen to Secretary of Treasury Robert Rubin and Alan Greenspan on critical matters.

The U.S. Economy Over the Next Decade

Always remember that the most difficult forecast to make is for the next day. Will selected interest rates go up or go down? Will futures prices for oil increase or decrease? Will the Dow Index plummet or skyrocket? You get the idea. If you are going to forecast, at least go out some fairly long length of time in order to let critical trends serve as barometric indicators of things to come.

At the moment the U.S. is the powerhouse of the world's economy and is, by far, the most dominant military force on earth. It's hard to imagine either of these changing for the next ten years. Maybe European Common Market will get its economic act together and begin to generate the per capita wealth numbers of the U.S., and the Asian economies, notably China, can grow significantly of they follow free-market, sound-money policies.

While the U.S. won't likely start a major war, the country could be drawn into some (nuclear) conflict (India-Pakistan, China-Taiwan). Table 7.4 lists U.S. wars since the American Revolution, and a certain periodicity about them is obvious. These wars led to sizable portions of young adult males dying and setting off demographic ripples for decades. They left a lasting impression on the far greater number of participants. They also led to some of the most harmful economic legislation on record. For simplicity in forecasting and hope in life, let's assume no big U.S. wars over the next decade.

Chapter 7

Table 7.4: U.S. Wars Since Colonial Times

American Revolution (1775-1784)
Participants-290,000
Deaths in service- 4,000

War of 1812
Participants-287,000
Deaths in service-2,000

Indian Wars (Approximately 1817-98)
Participants- 106,000
Deaths in service- 1,000

Mexican Wars (1846-1848)
Participants- 79,000
Deaths in service-13,000

Civil War (1861-1865)
Participants (Union)-2,213,000
Deaths in service (Union)-364,000
Participants (Confederate)- 1,000,000
Deaths in service (Confederate)-133,821

Spanish-American War (1898-1902)
Participants-392,000
Deaths in service- 11,000

World War I (1917-1918)
Participants-4,744,000
Deaths in service- 116,000
Living Veterans- 4,800

World War II (1940-1947)
Participants-16,535,000
Deaths in service-406,000
Living Veterans-6,319,000

Korean Conflict (1950-1955)
Participants-6,807,000
Deaths in service-55,000
Living veterans-4,179,000

Vietnam Era (1964-1975)
Participants-9,200,000
Deaths in service-109,000
Living veterans-8,166,000

Gulf War Era (1990-present)
Participants-3,800,000
Deaths in service-9,000
Living veterans-2,048,000

America's Wars Total (Through July 1, 1998)
War participants-41,790,000
Deaths in service-1,090,200
Living war veterans-19,300,000
Living ex-service members-25,188,000

Source: U.S. Veterans Administration

Let's assume as well that the global age is here and that foreign trade worldwide will continue to flourish. The World Trade Organization (WTO) serves as an effective means to handle global trade disputes and to push for the elimination of tariffs, quotas, and onerous regulations. The Internet guarantees that resources will move more efficiently around the world, ignoring traditional borders in the process, as long as Internet taxes are zero.

With these assumptions in mind, the standard starting place to look for future numbers is the *Blue Chip Consensus Forecast.* Here are 52 of the best macro gurus, and they rely extensively upon sophisticated econometric models used in conjunction with other forecasting techniques. Table 7.5 presents the consensus forecasts from the month of January since 1988, Alan Greenspan's time at the Fed. January forecasts for real GDP growth are given for the year in question and for the following year. The actual growth rates for the years in question are listed as well.

The consensus forecasts hardly inspire confidence. Only in 1990 and 1991 are the forecasts in January close to the actual year-end numbers for the year in question. The mean absolute error is 1.1 or 35 percent of the actual growth rate average. And it's even worse for the following year forecasts. Only in 1989 for 1990 and 1994 for 1995 are the forecasts on target, and the mean absolute error is 1.3 or 4.2 percent of the actual growth rate average.

Table 7.5: Blue Chip Consensus Real GDP Growth Rate
Forecasts In January: 1988-2000

	Forecast for The year	Forecast for The following Year	Actual GDP Growth the Year
Jan-88	2.2	2.1	4.2
Jan-89	2.7	1.7	3.5
Jan-90	1.7	2.2	1.7
Jan-91	-0.1	2.5	-0.2
Jan-92	1.6	3.1	3.3
Jan-93	2.9	3.2	2.4
Jan-94	3.0	2.7	4.0
Jan-95	3.1	2.2	2.7
Jan-96	2.2	2.2	3.7
Jan-97	2.3	2.1	4.5
Jan-98	2.5	2.3	4.3
Jan-99	2.4	2.3	4.0
Jan-00	3.6	3.0	

Source: Blue Chip Consensus
Forecasts, annual data.

From 1996 to 1999 both sets of forecasts were consistently below the actual numbers. The Blue Chip crowd in total was obviously having problems adjusting to the idea of the *New Economy*, in which growth would now be 4+ percent rather than the 2.5 percent per year seemed to accept as the potential until recently.

What about M₂ growth? After remaining below 5 percent a year from 1990 to 1996, it accelerated to nearly 9 percent in 1998. In the fall of 1998, the Fed engineered a series of short-run rate declines, in large part to stabilize the economy in the wake of the Asian currency and Russian crisis plus the problems with Long Term Capital Management. Similar to the stock market crash of 1987, the Fed under Greenspan readily stepped as the lender of last resort.

The rapid increase in M₂ continued until late October 1999, when annualized growth from the previous October remained over 6.5 percent. Of course, we hard-core monetarists pleaded for the Fed to slow M₂ growth down. And it certainly put forth an effort.

From June, 1999, to April, 2000, the Fed raised its federal funds rate target five quarter-point steps to the current level of 6 percent.

M$_2$ growth has, in conjunction, remained under 6 percent for the past five months. Real GDP growth the 4th quarter of 1999 was over 7 percent, and 1st quarter 2000 projections, are running 5+ percent. The Fed is expected to raise short-term rates a half-point increase at its next meeting, a move that will further show the growth of M$_2$.

You can now understand why, next to a war or a collapse in international trade, my biggest fear is that Alan Greenspan does not serve out his full term. What if someone is appointed who is a dove on inflation and believes that rapid monetary growth is necessary to maintain full employment over the business cycle?!

Another threat to the economy centers on the complexity of modern-day financial derivatives and the huge leverage they create. Even Alan Greenspan admits he doesn't understand what might happen if things here come tumbling in. Will the Fed still be able to function effectively as the lender of last resort?

A last concern is that the positive, go-to-it attitude that has dominated the U.S. national psyche the past 20 years somehow disappears. Jimmy Carter worried about a "malaise" in society, and this reasoning shaped attitudes about growth and potential productivity at the time. Poor economic leadership form the White House can quickly overwhelm many plus factors to set in motion "vicious cycles" rather "virtuous spirals."

All items considered, I must agree with Harry Dent and the other optimists who believe that the present upturn can last until at least 2008. Baby boomer spending seems quite likely to continue as the most potent injection in both the U.S. and world economies. In addition, we are in the midst of the "creative" part of another Schumpeter business cycle. The communications revolution is hitting the world at literally light speed as "unlimited" bandwidth opens up incredible new opportunities to transmit sounds, data and pictures. Hayek's flows of useful knowledge, so critical for the efficiency, are being magnified multifold at the moment.

Indeed, I don't see why the general prosperity of the U.S. over the past twenty years has to change fundamentally in 2008. Longer life expectancies and improved health conditions among the 60+ crowd lead me to think that baby boomers will mot start pulling large amounts of money out of the stock market at that time. Plus the investment-mentality is sweeping the generation X'ers and Y'ers, and I see them at least as aggressive as boomers in playing financial markets. Prosperity and strong growth can continue as long as monetary and fiscal policies are sound, and economists today have a far better idea of just what "sound" means than at any point since 1946. It is a time for great hope.

Closing Comments

We have covered a lot of ground in this book, from core micro foundations to the thicket of macro theories and forecasting. You certainly appreciate why modern economics is like a jigsaw puzzle that requires precision in putting the pieces together.

With the language and pictures of economics that you now possess, you can read extensively in professional business journals on a wide range of issues that impact your life. You can engage in meaningful conversations about particular economic problems. You can vote more astutely. And you will never be tricked by the word "free" again, a truly invaluable lesson for this world.

But even with the common language, common pictures, and relatively widespread macro agreement at the moment, you must go back to the fundamental theme made at the beginning of the book. Economists will never agree completely, certainly some economists are far more insightful than others. To help you remember this point, let me conclude with one last tale:

A man in a bar says to three guys: "You want to hear an economist joke?" "Well," said one, "I'm a former rugby player on the University of Chicago economics' department all-league champions. My friend here is a weightlifting gold medallist from the MIT economics' department. And my other friend started at middle linebacker while beginning his Ph.D. work at Sanford. Are you sure you still want to tell that economist joke?" "Well, shoot," says the first man. "Not if I have to explain it three times."

BIBLIOGRAPHY

Arrow, Kenneth. *Social Choice and Individual Values*. New York: Wiley, 1951.

Becker, Gary. "An Economic Analysis of Fertility" in *Demographic and Economic Change in Developed Countries*. Conference of the Universities – National Bureau Committee for Economic Research, Princeton, NJ: Princeton University Press, 1960.

Becker, Gary. "A Theory of the Allocation of Time." *Economic Journal*, September, 1965.

Becker, Gary. "A Note on Restaurant Pricing and Other Examples of Social Influences on Price." *Journal of Political Economy*, October, 1991.

Bernstein, Peter. *Against the Gods: The Remarkable Story of Risk*. New York: Wiley, 1996.

Blue Chip Economic Indicators, Panel Publishers: Alexandria, VA, various months.

Böhm-Bawerk, Eugene. *Capital and Interest*, 3 vol., reprinted Libertarian Press, Illinois, 1959. Translated by William Smart. New York: The Macmillan Co, 1890.

Boyes, William and Stephen Happel. "Auctions as an Allocation Mechanism in Academia: The Case of Faculty Offices." *Journal of Economic Perspectives*, Summer, 1989.

Chamberlin, E.H. *The Theory of Monopolistic Competition*, 1st ed. Cambridge, Mass.: Harvard University Press, 1933.

Coase, Ronald. "The Nature of the Firm." *Economica*, November, 1937.

Coase, Ronald. "The Problem of Social Cost." *Journal of Law and Economics*, October, 1960.

Darwin, Charles. *On the Origin of Species by Means of Natural Selection, or the Preservation of Favored Races in the Struggle for Life*. London: J. Murray, 1859.

Dent, Harry Jr. *The Great Boom Ahead*. New York: Hyperion, 1993.

Dent, Harry Jr. *The Roaring 2000's*. Cleveland: Simon and Schuster, 1998.

Dewald, William. "Inflation: Always a Monetary Phenomenon." *Monetary Trends*, The Federal Reserve Bank of St. Louis. October, 1997.

Eatwell, John, Murray Milgate, and Peter Newman (eds). *The New Palgrave: The World of Economics*. New York: Norton, 1991.

Epstein, Gene. "Mr. Market: An Interview with Milton Friedman." *Barron's*, August 24, 1998.

Economic Report of the President. U.S. Government Printing Office, Washington, D.C., 1988.

Economic Report of the President. U.S. Government Printing Office, Washington, D.C., 2000.

Farris, Martin and Stephen Happel. *Modern Managerial Economics.* Glenview: Scott Foresman, 1987.

Ferguson, C.E. *Microeconomic Theory.* Homewood: Richard D. Irwin, 1966.

Fisher, Irving. *The Rate of Interest.* New York: The Macmillan Co., 1907.

Fisher, Irving. *The Theory of Interest: As Determined by Impatience to Spend Income and Opportunity to Invest It.* New York: The Macmillan Co., 1930.

Friedman, Milton. "The Methodology of Positive Economics." *Essays in Positive Economics.* Chicago: The University of Chicago Press, 1953.

Friedman, Milton. *A Theory of the Consumption Function.* Princeton: Princeton University Press, 1957.

Friedman, Milton. *Capitalism and Freedom.* Chicago: The University of Chicago Press, 1962.

Friedman, Milton. "The Role of Monetary Policy." *American Economic Review.* March, 1968.

Friedman, Milton. "The Fed and the Natural Rate." *Wall Street Journal.* September 24, 1996.

Friedman, Milton, and Anna Schwartz. *A Monetary History of the United States, 1867-1960.* National Bureau of Economic Research, Princeton, NJ, 1963.

Galbraith, John. *The Affluent Society.* Boston: Houghton Mifflin, 1958.

Galbraith, John. *Money: Whence It Came, Where It Went.* Boston: Houghton Mifflin, 1975.

Gordon, Robert. *The American Business Cycle: Continuity and Change.* Chicago: The University of Chicago Press, 1986.

Hansen, Alvin. *A Guide to Keynes.* New York: McGraw-Hill, 1953.

Happel, Stephen and Marianne Jennings. "Herd Them Together and Scalp Them." *Wall Street Journal,* February 23, 1995.

Hayek, F.A. *The Road to Serfdom.* Chicago: The University of Chicago Press, 1944.

Hayek, F.A. "The Use of Knowledge in Society." *American Economic Review,* September, 1945.

Bibliography

Hicks, John. "Mr. Keynes and the 'Classics', A Suggested Interpretation." *Econometrica*, April, 1937.

Kaza, Greg. "Is There a Case for the Gold Standard?" *The Intercollegiate Review*, Fall, 1996.

Keynes, John Maynard. *The Economic Consequences of Peace*. New York: Harcourt, Brace, and Howe, 1920.

Keynes, John Maynard. *The Economic Consequences of Mr. Churchill*. New York: Harcourt, Brace, and Howe, 1925.

Keynes, John Maynard. *The General Theory of Employment, Interest, and Money*. London: Macmillan, 1936.

Keynes, John Maynard. "The General Theory." *Quarterly Journal of Economics*, February, 1937.

Klamer, Arjo. *Conversations with Economists*. Totowa, NJ: Rowman and Allanheld, 1983.

Kuhn, W.E. *The Evolution of Economic Thought* (2nd ed). Cincinnati: South-Western, 1970.

Kuznets, Simon. "National Income" in *Encyclopedia of Social Sciences*, 1933. Reprinted in *Readings in the theory of Income Distribution*, W. Fellner and B. F. Haley (eds.). Philadelphia: Blakiston for American Economic Association, 1946.

Lucas, Robert. "Econometric Policy Evaluation: A Critique," in Karl Brunner and A. H. Meltzer (eds.), *The Phillips Curve and Labor Markets*, supplement to the *Journal of Monetary Econmics*, 1976.

Malthus, Thomas R. *An Essay on the Principle of Population, As It Affects The Future Improvement in Society. With Remarks on the Speculations of Mr. Godwin, Mr. Condorcet, and Other Writers*. London: J. Johnson, 1798.

Malthus, Thomas R. *Principles of Political Economy, Considered with a View to Their Practical Application*, London: J. Murray, 1820.

Marshall, Alfred. *Principles of Economics*. London: Macmillan, 1890.

Marx, Karl. *Capital: A Critique of Political Economy* (edited by Frederick Engels). London: Swan Sonnenschien, Lowry, and Co. English edn, 1887, German edn, 1867.

Marx, Karl and Friedrich Engels. *The Communist Manifesto*. New York: New York Labor News Co., 1848.

Menger, Carl. *Principles of Economics*. Translated by James Dingwall and Bert F. Hoselitz, Wien: W. Braumuller, 1871.

Mises, Ludwig. *Human Action: A Treatise on Economics*. Chicago: Regnery, 1949.

Modigliani, Franco. "The Life Cycle Hypothesis of Saving, the Demand for Wealth, and the Supply of Capital." *Social Research*, 1966.

Muth, J. F. "Rational Expectations and the Theory of Price Movements." *Econometrica*, July, 1961.

Neumann, John and Oscar Morgenstern. *Theory of Games and Economic Behavior*. Princeton: Princeton University Press, 1944.

Phillips, A. W. "The Relation Between Unemployment and the Rate of Change of Money Wages in the United Kingdom, 1961-1957." *Economica*, November, 1958.

Pigou, C.A. *The Economics of Welfare*. London: Macmillan, 1920.

Rand, Ayn. *The Fountainhead*. Indianapolis: Bobs-Merrill, 1943.

Rand, Ayn. *Atlas Shrugged*. New York: Random House, 1957.

Ricardo, David. *Principles of Political Economy and Taxation*. London: Dent, 1817.

Robinson, Joan. *The Economics of Imperfect Competition*. London: Macmillan, 1933.

Samuelson, Paul. *The Foundations of Economic Analysis*. Cambridge: Harvard University Press, 1947.

Samuelson, Paul. *Economics*. New York: McGraw-Hill, various editions (1st edn, 1948).

Sargent, Thomas, and Wallace, Neil. "The Real-Bills Doctrine versus the Quantity Theory: A Reconsideration." *Journal of Political Economy*, December, 1982.

Schumpeter, Joseph. *Business Cycles*. New York: McGraw-Hill, 1939.

Schumpeter, Joseph. *Capitalism, Socialism and Democracy*. New York: Harper, 1942.

Smith, Adam. *The Theory of Moral Sentiments* (edited by D.D. Raphael and A. L. Macfie from the 6th edition of 1790). Oxford: Oxford University Press, 1976 (1st edn, 1759).

Smith, Adam. *An Inquiry into the Nature and Causes of the Wealth of Nations* (edited by Edwin Cannan). New York: Random House, Modern Library Edition, 1937 (Originally published by W. Strahan and T. Cadell: London, 1776).

Solow, Robert. "A Contribution to the Theory of Economic Growth." *Quarterly Journal of Economics*, February, 1956.

Bibliography

Spengler, Joseph. *Population Economics: Selected Essays* (Compiled by Robert Smith, Frank de Vyver, and William Allen). Durham: Duke University Press, 1972.

Staley, Charles. *A History of Economic Thought: From Aristotle to Arrow*. Cambridge: Blackwell, 1991.

Stigler, George. *The Citizen and the State: Essays on Regulation*. Chicago: The University of Chicago Press, 1975.

Sweezy, Paul. "Demand Under Conditions of Oligopoly." *Journal of Political Economy*, August, 1939.

Timberlake, Richard. *Monetary Policy in the United States: An Intellectual and Institutional History*. Chicago: The University of Chicago Press, 1993.

Tobin, James. "Monetary Theory: New and Old Looks." *American Economic Review*, May, 1961.

U.S. Bureau of the Census. Current Population Reports *Projections of the Population of the United States by Age, Sex, and Race: 1990-2080* (Series P-25, No. 1018), 1989.

U.S. Bureau of the Census. Current Population Reports *Population Projections of the United States by Age, Sex, Race, and Hispanic Origin: 1995-2050* (Series P-25, No. 1030), 1996.

U.S. Financial Data, The Federal Reserve of St. Louis, various weeks, 1998.

Wanniski, Jude. "The Optimal Price of Gold." *Wall Street Journal*, January 7, 1998.

Webster's New World Dictionary (2nd College ed.). Cleveland: Simon and Schuster, 1984.

Weintraub, E. Roy. *Microfoundations: The Compatibility of Microeconomics and Macroeconomics*. Cambridge: Cambridge University Press, 1979.

Wieser, Friedrich. *Natural Value*. Translated by Christian A. Malloch. New York: Kelley & Millman, Inc, 1956.

SUBJECT INDEX

Adam Smith and the Classical School, 120
Adaptive expectations, 142
Animal spirits, 133
ARMA/ARIMA models, 162
Auctions to allocate faculty office, 46-52
Austrian School, 148-150
Average product of labor, 24
Baby-Boom Generation, 170
Banking Act of 1933, 97
Banking Act of 1935, 94, 98
Banking Holding Act (1956), 101
Barometric forecasting techniques, 162
Barometric price leadership, 73
Barter, 82
Basil Accords (1988), 102
Being at the margin, 21
Blue Chip consensus forecasts, 187
Board of Governors of Fed, 94
Bourgeoisie, 124
Bretton Woods agreements, 99, 100, 138
Bush years, 183-184
Capital consumption allowance, 107
Cartels, 12-13
Carter years, 180-181
Ceteris paribus, 11
Chicago School, 140-145
Chicago-Columbia approach to
    fertility, 57-59
    Rotten kid theorem, 58
Classical time series analysis, 161
Clayton Act (1914), 38
Clinton years, 184-185
Coase Theorem, 36-37
Coinage Act (1792), 87
Combined marginal revenue curve, 76
Community Reinvestment Act (1977),
    101-102
Compensated dollar, 131
Complements, 78-79
Comsumer sovereignty, 105
Continentals, 86-87
Corn Law debates, 122
Costs
    Average variable costs, 26
    Average fixed costs, 26
    Average costs, 27
    Marginal costs, 26-27

Council of Economic Advisor chairs,
    158-159
Council of Economic Advisors, 1
Country pay, 86
Creative destruction, 39-41
Crime of 1873, 91
Day-to-day knowledge, 42
Demand (Law of), 28-29
Demand for money, 113
Demographics in the U.S., 166-172
    Working age groups, 167
    Older age groups, 169
    Three generations, 170-171
    Harry Dent's demographics, 171-172
Depository Institutions Deregulations
    Act (1980), 100, 102
Diminishing Physical Returns
    (Law of), 24
Discount rate, 93
Discouraged workers, 111
Dismal science, 1
Disposable Income (DY), 109
Division and specialization of labor, 9
Dominant price leadership, 73
Double coincidence of wants, 82
Early American Keynesians, 136-139
Econometric modeling, 163, 164
Economic conservatives, 119-120
Economic liberals, 118-119
Economics, 3
Eisenhower years, 176-177
Elasticity of price, 61
    Factors affecting, 64-65
Equation of Exchange, 113
Equilibrium, 32
    General equilibrium, 39
Equimarginalism, 22
Excess capacity theorem, 71
Expenditure approach to GDP, 106-107
Externality, 35
    Benefit externalities, 35
    Cost externalities, 35
FDIC Improvement Act (1992), 102
Fallacy of composition, 12
Favorable balance of trade, 8
Fed-Treasury Accord of 1951, 99, 101
Federal Deposit Insurance
    Corporation (FDIC), 97

Subject Index

Federal Open Market Committee
(FOMC), 94-95, 98
Federal Reserve, 92-95
  Chairs of Fed, 95
Federal funds rate, 93
Fiat currency, 84
Financial Institutions Reform,
  Recovery, and Enforcement
  Act (1989), 102
First Bank of the United States, 87
Fisher equation (Fisher effect), 132
Flow variables, 31
Food and Drug Administration, 43
Fractionally-backed currency, 84
Free as a dangerous word, 13-14
Free banking, 89
Free markets, 15
Free trade, 9, 15
Frictional unemployment, 111
Full cost pricer, 77
Full gold standard, 91-92
Full price, 57
Full-bodied coins, 84
Fully-backed currency, 84
Functional finance, 134
Game theory, 72
  Zero-sum game, 72
General equilibrium, 39
Generation X, 170
Generation Y, 170-171
Glass-Steagall provisions, 97, 101
Gold Coin Act (1834), 89
Gold Reserve Act (1934), 97
Gold Standard Act
  (Currency Act) (1900), 91
Government-regulated monopoly, 38-39
Greenbacks, 90-91
Gresham's Law, 88
Gross Domestic Prodcut (GDP), 105
Gross National Prodcut (GNP), 105
Humphrey-Hawkins Act (1978), 102
Income approach to GDP, 107-108
Incremental pricer, 77
Indirect business taxes, 108
Inferior goods, 57
Injections, 128
International Monetary Fund (IMF), 99
Inventors vs. innovators, 41
Invisible hand, 10
Involuntary unemployment, 111
Iron Law of Wages, 25, 122

John Bates Clark Medal
  recipients, 155-157
Kennedy-Johnson years, 177-178
Kinked demand curve, 63-64, 72-73
Labor theory of value, 8-9
Labor-saving technology, 124
Laffer Curve, 146-147
Law of Demand, 28-29
Law of Diminishing Physical Returns, 24
Law of Opportunity Costs, 22
Law of Supply, 29-30
Leading indicators
  for the U.S. economy, 162
Leakages, 128
Liquidity trap, 134
Long run in production, 21
Macroeconomics, 11
Malthusian population theory, 122
Marginal, 20
Marginal costs, 20
Marginal efficiency of capital, 134
Marginal product of labor, 24-25
Marginal productivity
  principle of distribution, 129
Marginal revenue, 20
  Combined marginal revenue curve, 76
Market period, 21
Market shortage, 33-34
Market surplus, 33-34
Marx's stages of
  economic systems, 123-126
  Full communism, 125
Mechanical extrapolation, 161
Mercantilism, 8
Monetarism, 141-143
Monetary Reform Act (1980), 100, 102
Money illusion, 110
Money stock of U.S., 102-105
  M_1, M_2, M_3, MZM, L, 103-104
  Legal reserves, 104
  Monetary base, 104
Money, 82-83
  As medium of exchange, 82
  As standard of value, 83
  As store of value, 83
Monopolies of the Crown, 8
Monopolistic competition, 69
Monopoly, 73-76
  Pure, 73
  Natural, 38
  Comparison to pure competition, 37-38

Moral hazards, 14
Most efficient point of production, 27
National Banking Act (1863), 90
National Income (NY), 107-109
Natural monopolies, 38
Natural rate of unemployment, 142
Negative spillover effects, 35
Neighborhood effects, 35
Neoclassical synthesis, 137
Nixon-Ford years, 179-180
Nobel Prize recipients
    in economics, 151-154
Nominal GDP vs. real GDP, 109-110
Normal goods, 57
Normal profits, 39
Office of the Comptroller of the
    Currency (OCC), 90
Oligopoly, 71
Open market operations, 93
Opportunity cost, 22
Paradox of majority voting, 13
Paradox of thrift, 13-14
Pareto optimal, 165
Penetration pricing, 78
Perfect competition, 41
Personal Income (PY), 109
Phillips curve, 137-139
Pigou effect, 130
Plant, 24
Post-Eclectic Keynesians, 139-140
Presidential administration
    outcomes since 1946, 173-185
Price control (ceiling), 33
Price discrimination, 74-76
    First degree, 75-76
    Second degree, 76
    Third degree, 76
Price elasticity, 61-62
    Unitary elastic, 63
    Perfectly inelastic, 63
    Perfectly elastic, 64
    In relation to MR, 65-66
Price support (floor), 34
Price theory, 129
Prisoners' Dilemma, 12, 71-72
Products
    Total output (product), 25
    Average product of labor, 25
    Marginal product of labor, 25-26
Proletariat, 124
Public good, 36

Pure competition, 41, 68-69
Pure monopoly, 73-74
Pure monopoly, 73-74
Rational expectations, 145-146
Rational marginalist, 21-22
Reagan years, 181-183
Real bill of exchange, 10
Real cash balances, 131
Real wealth effect, 130
Real-bills doctrine, 85-86
Relative price, 28
Reserve army of unemployment, 124
Reserve requirements, 93
Resolution Trust Corporation (RTC), 100
Riegle-Neil Interstate Banking and
    Branching Efficiency Act (1994), 102
Rotten-kid theorem, 58
Say's Law, 112, 128
Scientific knowledge, 42
Seigniorage, 84, 88
Sherman Act (1890), 38
Short run in production, 21
Simple Money Rule, 143-144
Skimming, 78
Smithsonian Agreement (1971), 101
Social deviants, 39
St. Germain-Garn Act (1982), 102
Stock variables, 31
Structural unemployment, 111
Substitutes, 78-79
Sunk costs, 23
Supply-side economics, 146-148
Survey techniques, 162-163
Ticket scalping, 53-56
Token coins, 84
Total output, 24
Tragedy of the commons, 12
Transfer pricing, 79-80
Truman years, 175-176
U.S. road market, 44-45
Utility, 27-28
Utils, 27-28, 148
Velocity of money, 113
Very long run in production, 21
Wars in the U.S., 186
Water-diamond paradox, 8-9, 28
Wildcat banking, 89
World Bank, 99
Zero-sum game, 72

AUTHOR INDEX

Ackley, Gardner, 158
Allais, Maurice, 153
Arrow, Kenneth, 13, 151, 155
Baily, Martin, 140, 159
Barro, Robert, 145
Becker, Gary, 57, 153, 156
Bertrand, Joseph, 71
Blinder, Alan, 140
Boskin, Michael, 159
Boulding, Kenneth, 155
Boyes, William, 46
Brunner, Karl, 141
Buchanan, James, 153
Burns, Arthur, 158
Böhm-Bawerk, Eugene, 131, 148
Calvin, John, 2, 8
Card, David, 157
Chamberlain, E.H., 69
Churchill, Winston, 115, 118
Coase, Ronald, 36, 153
Copeland, Aaron, 1
Cournot, Augustine, 71
Darwin, Charles, 123
Debreu, Gerald, 152
Degas, Edgar, 60
Dent, Harry, 171-172
Edgeworth, F.Y., 71
Ehrlich, Paul, 122-123
Eisner, Robert, 140
Engels, Friedrich, 123
Feldstein, Martin, 156, 159
Fischer, Stanley, 140
Fisher, Franklin, 156
Fisher, Irving, 131
Fogel, Robert, 153
Friedman, Milton, 140-145, 152, 155
Frisch, Ragnar, 151
Galbraith, John Kenneth, 136-137, 160
Greenspan, Alan, 150, 159
Griliches, Zvi, 156
Grossman, Sanford, 157
Haavelmo, Trygve, 153
Hansen, Alvin, 136
Happel, Stephen, 46, 53
Harrod, Roy, 133
Harsanyi, John, 72, 153
Hausman, Jerry, 157
Hayek, F.A., 42-43, 149, 151

Heckman, James, 156
Heller, Walter, 138, 158
Hicks, John, 136, 151
Houthakker, Hendrik, 155
Jennings, Marianne, 53
Jevons, Stanley, 27
Jordon, Jerry, 141
Jorgenson, Dale, 156
Kantorovich, Leonid, 151
Keynes, John Maynard, 127, 132-136
Keyserling, Leon, 158
Klein, Lawrence, 136, 152, 155
Knight, Frank, 140
Koopmans, Tjalling, 151
Kreps, David, 157
Krugman, Paul, 140, 157
Kuznets, Simon, 105, 151
Laffer, Arthur, 146
Leontief, Wassily, 151
Lewis, Arthur, 152
Lucas, Robert, 145, 154
Malthus, Thomas, 25, 27, 122
Markowitz, Harry, 153
Marshall, Alfred
    Biographical sketch, 19-20
Marx, Karl, 27
McCracken, Paul, 158
McFadden, Daniel, 156
Meade, James, 152
Meltzer, Alan, 141
Menger, Carl, 27, 123, 148
Merton, Robert, 154
Miller, Merton, 153
Mirrlees, James, 72, 154
Mises, Ludwig, 148
Modigliani, Franco, 137, 152
Morgenstern, Oskar, 72
Mundell, Robert, 146, 154
Murphy, Kevin, 157
Muth, John, 145
Myrdal, Gunnar, 151
Nash, John, 72, 153
Neumann, John von, 72
Newton, Isaac, 2
Ohlin, Bertil, 152
Patton, George S., 18
Phillips, A.W., 137
Pigou, C.A., 130

Poe, Edgar Allen, 165
Rand, Ayn, 150
Reagan, Ronald, 119
Reynolds, Alan, 147
Ricardo, David, 122
Robinson, Joan, 69, 133
Rukeyser, Louis, 160
Samuelson, Paul, 136, 151, 155
Sargent, Thomas, 145
Saulnier, Raymond, 158
Savant, Marilyn vos, 81
Say, Jean-Baptiste, 112
Scholes, Myron, 154
Schultz, Theodore, 152
Schultze, Charles, 159
Schumpeter, Joseph, 7-8, 39-41, 148-149
Schwartz, Anna, 141
Selten, Reinhard, 72, 153
Sen, Amartya, 154
Sharpe, William, 153
Sheifer, Andrei, 157
Simon, Herbert, 152
Smith, Adam, 2, 5, 7-10, 27,
    36-37, 42, 84-86, 112
    Biographical sketch, 6-7
Solow, Robert, 153, 155
Spence, Michael, 156
Sprinkel, Beryl, 159
Stein, Herbert, 158
Stigler, George, 7, 152
Stiglitz, Joseph, 140, 156, 159
Stone, Richard, 152
Summers, Lawrence, 140, 157
Sweezy, Paul, 72, 126
Thurow, Lester, 140
Tinbergen, Jan, 151
Tobin, James, 137, 152, 155
Tyson, Laura, 140, 159
Vickrey, William, 72, 154
Wallace, Neil, 145
Wanniski, Jude, 146
Weidenbaum, Murray, 159
Wieser, Fredrick, 148
Yellen, Janet, 159